Job

Interviews

The Ultimate Resource to Get the Job You Really Want

(How to Face the Behavioral Interview With Preparation to Relax and Overcome the Job Interview)

William Ortiz

Published By **Chris David**

William Ortiz

All Rights Reserved

Job Interviews: The Ultimate Resource to Get the Job You Really Want (How to Face the Behavioral Interview With Preparation to Relax and Overcome the Job Interview)

ISBN   978-1-998927-08-1

Published By **Chris David**

ISBN   978-1-998927-08-1

Legal & Disclaimer

Table Of Contents

Chapter 1: Understanding the Unspoken Interview Question

The interview is the right venue to introduce yourself as a person likeable, defend your alternatives and beyond selections, sell your research and achievements and in the end, persuade the interviewer which you are the right desire that he/she will in no manner remorse choosing. For many humans, the effects of the interviews are decided through resume and eloquence; in fact, for loads times, they're accurate.

It is not any thriller that maximum those who go through interviews fail. Rejection is greater commonplace than approval. Sometimes, even being the second extraordinary just won't do. The necessities for interviews have end up better and better that humans have already forgotten to cope with the hidden interview query.

Establishing a reference to the interviewer is the real clincher. No large enjoy have to make him receive as true with you and no fulfillment ought to make him cushty speakme with you if a link is lacking. It is easy to assert such plenty of topics, however if you do no longer meet with the interviewer eye to eye, your application will sincerely be every other overachiever candidate who can not surpass the remaining level of connection – trust.

Connection is not as easy as speaking to someone. You can talk all day; but if the other person isn't always worried to begin with, there will in no way be reciprocity. Likewise, you may talk effectively; however without incomes his consider, your goal for having that interview will not going be met.

To understand what the real magic connection is all about, you need to recognize first the 4 ranges of connection and attempt to surpass they all. They have come to be hobby, developing an splendid impact, stimulating hobby and hobby, and earning the trust. Successfully surpassing all tiers is the handiest time even as you may actually claim which you have made a connection.

1. Getting hobby

Getting hobby thru outrageous strategies almost constantly works. However, the form of hobby it receives now not regularly produces first rate final effects, so in location of in search of to be specific in an retro way, reason to meet the popularity quo or turn out to be brilliant.

Stick to the requirements. The interviewer ought to see which you are able to conform. You additionally need to manipulate but now not suppress your individual specially if it may make a right communique look too awkward. Charisma will help you get started out.

2. Creating an notable affect

This is the effect of exuding air of thriller. Leaving a extremely good effect is based upon at the proper tendencies that you display at some degree within the interview, built thru proper gestures and frame language that make your characteristics seem innate. Saying some thing exceptional could probable get the interviewer's interest, but you may excellent create an amazing and lasting have an effect on thru helping it via your moves and manner of speakme.

For example, claiming which you are correct in presentation conforms to their necessities. However, if you may not be capable of gift your self impressively within the the the front of the interviewer, your claim may be counted as not whatever but whole irony. That is the impact you'll get.

Getting a person's attention and growing a splendid have an effect on is form of always straight away if you have all the right functions. However, in an interview set-up, interviewers are skilled no longer to recollect a few aspect they pay interest and observe to your resume with out getting clues of what you have to provide first.

3. Stimulating interest and curiosity

In an interview, stimulating interest and interest handiest relates to as a minimum one difficulty — your capacity to make the interviewer need to investigate extra approximately you and what you want to provide. Introducing yourself thru mentioning what you have were given honestly written on your resume inspires boredom and at that very 2d, you have got already did no longer stimulate interest.

On the alternative hand, introducing your self via declaring what makes you the best candidate for the position can pique the interviewer's hobby and curiosity. Remember that an interviewer wishes a person who knows what he dreams and what he can do.

There is not any one-of-a-kind manner to head beyond this level, but through imparting substance. By the prevent of the interview, you need to have been able to benefit mutual hobby.

four. Earning the keep in mind

This is wherein rapport is available in. This is the factor in which it isn't sufficient to actually speak to an interviewer; you have got were given to speak with him. After stimulating the interviewer's hobby, you need to be that specialize in making him recall in you via appearing credible and dependable. You want to open up your self, certainly so he can see via the whole thing you say.

You will have a look at what rapport way inside the succeeding bankruptcy.

Chapter 2: How to Improve your Charisma

Let's get you organized with the primary device to connect with the interviewer nonverbally or subconsciously... Charisma.

Charisma is defined as "specific magnetic appeal or enchantment." Although physical beauty does not say the whole lot, it does make contributions substantially to air of mystery. Who isn't appealing to neat and proper seems except?

When you invest for your appears, you moreover might also additionally put money into your future due to the fact the physical detail of your character leaves a first-rate effect. The have an impact on of mind and character to the give up result of an interview can in no way be overstated. However, it is very critical which you do no longer handiest popularity at the internal, but additionally what is at the out of doors.

When Prince modified into no matter the fact that starting his recording profession in the

7

past due 70s, his first album emerge as now not exactly what you may call a enterprise fulfillment. However, greater than that sadness, it modified into his loss of aura that made the executives from Warner cancel his tour. He come to be already a splendid musician whilst a amateur, a musical genius at that, however his first performances lacked attraction to maintain humans purchasing his live suggests and preserve manufacturers taking a risk on this hitherto small musical decide.

A three hundred and sixty five days after, Prince came returned with a current photo and emblem, the quirky little Prince whom people nevertheless understand to nowadays − normal however captivating. He changed into not genuinely growing a music, but appearing and charming audiences anywhere within the u.S.. Many critics function his rise to repute to his witty appeal that is additionally now visible inside the likes of Lady Gaga and Katy Perry. His air of thriller without a doubt made up for his pinnacle and extra appropriate his musicality by way of manner of dozens of times.

There are times at the same time as charisma compensates for masses of things, serving as a alternative outstanding even as human beings fall brief of competencies, competencies, proper seems and cloth possessions. You can say that it solves greater than half of of the photograph and attraction trouble that many human beings have. In Prince's case, charisma protected insecurities and changed them with oozing self-self belief.

The equal is actual for Britney Spears, who might have been missing vocal understanding, however makes up for it with teeming charisma, pushing her to the ranks of pop princesses and recording royalties. Her aura gave her self warranty to grow to be an all-time favourite pop vocalist (many critics remember it as one in each of the maximum essential ironies of the leisure enterprise), who although acting in lip synch (that is what she is well-known for) however delivered performances with conviction.

As an interviewee, you are there now not most effective to have an effect on however moreover captivate your very critical target marketplace that is the interviewer. You need to sell your qualifications because of the reality most of the time, they do now not talk for themselves. It isn't always enough to reveal what you can do, but you furthermore might also need to exude an entire lot of air of thriller to become memorable.

In this chapter, the development of air of mystery is probably divided into additives: the appeal and the attraction. The "appeal" element discusses the development of your character and disposition in dealing with situations and your self inside the the front of a crowd, even as the "appeal" issue tackles physical development in particular imagined to put together you for an interview.

Both are had to balance out your charisma and make certain that you do now not sincerely get the interviewer's interest but moreover his endure in thoughts.

Charm

1. Wear a huge smile

A authentic smile can with out problems uplift the temper of the grumpiest interviewer. It is contagious, . When you smile, you furthermore also can set off the opportunity individual to reciprocate and succeeding with that glaringly secures a connection.

In any business enterprise, human beings want to paintings and communicate with someone who appears clean to speak with and moderate to art work with. Almost every process in the world has a degree of stress, so the final problem an interviewer desires is to simply accept an applicant who might be competitive but annoying to be with.

Smiling magically opens up your self to a few different man or woman. It is like announcing "I am inviting you to understand me better" and certainly, the interviewer will oblige. It does now not say lots approximately your competency and it moreover does now not justify your qualifications; however it honestly highlights your person, a prerequisite to building receive as actual with.

If you're demanding approximately the interview, better cowl it with a smile. Just strain it. Getting used to it will make you experience higher (scientifically talking, forcing a grin is enough to growth your experience-top hormone known as endorphin), so you will be capable of characteristic greater as it should be.

ACTION TIME:

Please take motion on every occasion you be aware "ACTION TIME". There is no price in searching for this book if you do now not workout.It is like gaining knowledge of to swim... You have to look at a ebook on how to do the butterfly stroke however in case you do not bounce into the pool, there ain't no butterfly for you.

Here is the exercising:

Learn to put on the high-quality smile that is suitable for interview training.

Use your webcam and file a few smiling poses that you expect might be suitable.

Then deliver the video clip for your buddies community and ask them for comments. Ask them to pick the terrific smile that they pick, if they are interviewers.

Adopt the smile that has the most votes.

2. Always communicate with conviction

What does it in reality mean to speak with conviction? It truely technique believing the entirety you are pronouncing, regardless if you are not yet completely glad of it. Neophyte crook experts struggle this problem, however despite the fact that become reading the art work of speaking with conviction. Look at how all legal professionals claim that their customers are harmless however understanding that some of them are definitely accountable (otherwise, the area may be free of crimes).

You should don't forget your self first in advance than the interviewer can recall you. Speaking halfheartedly displays in your delivery. There is no air of secrecy in that. A hooked up manner to improve your conviction whilst speakme is through manner of schooling your organized advent and solutions over and over until they in the end become herbal to you (that is why it is not recommended to memorize your answers). Know every element of what you need to mention and the way to protect it.

ACTION TIME:

Please take motion whenever you spot "ACTION TIME".

Same manner right right here.

Record a video of your introduction and ask for feedback. Would your friends (as interviewers) revel in which you are actual, compassionate, enthusiastic, influential, natural and convincing after looking your short video clip?

OK, if you need to model or mimic (some other extremely good NLP device that you can quickly examine), go to YouTube and look for movies on debates or influential leaders and duplicate how they talk.

three. Communicate really

Positivity draws humans and spreading your powerful outlook can without issues assist you get the take delivery of as real with of the interviewer. It isn't unusual to pay interest horrific reviews in interviews. After all, the choice of most candidates to move in advance and find higher corporations to sign up for is commonly due to their terrible testimonies with their past employers. The actual challenge is a manner to make those testimonies appear immoderate extremely good.

Instead of griping over your former company's selfish manipulate patterns and the agency's meager benefits, inform the interviewer that you are looking for a few issue better with out constantly elucidating at the motives. Should he ask for unique reasons, be honest, however ensure to say a few high first-class angles much like the matters you've got were given found, your satisfactory coworkers or the prestige of the employer.

For instance, as opposed to pronouncing "I left the employer because of the truth they do no longer provide enough importance to their personnel" say "I in fact like my paintings as it allowed me to expand thru making use of my skills, however I determined to transport in advance with a few one of a kind organisation due to the reality my boss and I appear to have awesome priorities and dreams." The interviewer is aware of that there will constantly be variations in critiques and requirements in any enterprise agency; it's far most effective a depend of how human beings accept them.

ACTION TIME:

Please take motion on every occasion you spot "ACTION TIME".

For every day, listing down the feelings that you experience.

For examples, usually I might likely enjoy the subsequent: calm, peace, satisfaction, enthusiasm, disenchanted.

You will phrase that there are greater great feelings than terrible feelings.

Do this for a few days or a week and have a study your emotional pattern.

If you have got extra terrible feelings, then there may be a unethical that you could challenge negativity without you expertise it.

Likewise, when you have extra super emotions, then your great feelings can be projected on your surrounding place.

People may be more drawn inside the path of folks which is probably fantastic.

It may additionally additionally take you days or months to trade from being horrific to super.

In the period in-between, if you need to move for the interview, do your wonderful to live extremely good. Do something you enjoy the day earlier than you go for the interview to crank up your effective emotions.

4. Relate to some thing non-public

In maximum interviews, the topics best revolve round qualifications and expert increase (this is, bear in mind it or not, interpreted by means of the use of many interviewers as sales enhance). There are individuals who will harp on their abilties to regular a way even as there are those who will try and fawn with the aid of banking at the organization's popularity or the location's promising blessings. Joining those groups does now not growth your threat of getting the slot. Rather, it's far with the resource of displaying that you aren't a slave of industrialism and commercialism a very good manner to make you awesome (examine: boom isn't all about position and cash).

Adding private affection on your interview allow you to make a personal connection to the interviewer, likely tackling with the beneficial useful resource of danger a few difficulty this is also near his coronary coronary coronary heart. Whenever you're given the possibility, share how your circle of relatives, friends or dreams offer you with thought and motivation to artwork more hard. Share how failures and disappointments renewed you as someone and bolstered your remedy.

Sharing your inclined moments moreover hardly ever fails in getting sympathy. Just ensure you close up up up it with the beneficial resource of telling how you pulled via and bounced back higher. Nothing beats a private contact, so use it on your gain.

Appeal

1. Invest on your seems

So, what want to you do in case you aren't without a doubt gifted with a twiglet frame or an angelic face? Have a complete makeover.

This is in which dad and mom and functionality employers greatly variety from each specific. Parents provide unconditional love, a few factor that employers rarely have, so that is a first-rate time to ask for unbiased feedback for your look other than your mother and father' perennial compliments.

You need to invest in your seems because of the fact that may be your credential right there in the the front of the replicate. That does no longer suggest you need to sacrifice ability and mind, but also do now not underestimate the strength of beauty.

Physical beauty is a connection that many humans fail to make the maximum because of the fact they assume that it is too mundane and trivial. You do now not want to undergo a surgical procedure; but you want to be at your amazing in thoughts and frame.

ACTION TIME:

Let's move for a workout.

A few days earlier than the interview, begin hitting the gymnasium or exercise religiously. The purpose isn't precisely to shed kilos if you are a piece heavyweight, but to make you appear taut, leaner and more impregnable. Men with distinguished shoulders and chest are greater influential. Women with toned curves look greater dignified and responsible. You can be surprised how a few days of workout can enhance your bodily appearance considerably.

2. Choose the proper fashion assertion

You need to invest in cosmetic products and fashionable garments and add-ons. Learn a manner to conceal your impurities with makeup (many groups require their personnel to position on makeup). Nevertheless, make-up need to best be used to beautify physical look with the useful resource of searching natural as a good deal as possible. You are going to an interview and now not to a party. Know the distinction.

One big mistake ladies commit is going to an interview like they'll be approximately to enroll in a splendor competition. Although this could actually decorate their enchantment, it has a connotation that repels interviewers and future bosses alike.

In the place of business, the wrong use of make-up must make you look like someone who is making an attempt to make a deal with the resource of seduction. An interviewer will no longer choose someone who seems to be pushing a private time table in preference to a expert boom. Having an excessive amount of taking region on your face can also intimidate conservative interviewers.

Even men can advantage from expertise the way to use enough make-up. Concealer, foundation and bronzer may be beneficial in securing an approval.

Also, pick out out out clothes that reward your frame shape, size and pores and pores and pores and skin tone. Make sure that the clothes you placed on within the course of an interview additionally in form the agency's necessities and manner of lifestyles (i.E. In no manner located on a turtleneck if you are utilizing as a server in "Hooters"). Stick with subdued colours which consist of blue, green, grey, and brown and avoid carrying yellow (related to emotional detachment) and red (elicits awful emotions). Violet and orange also are top alternatives to growth emotional connection. Simply located, you need to get dressed for the event; but how will you recognize if you are deciding on the proper clothes?

Chapter 3: Connecting Using Body Movements and Gestures

Your body moves and gestures can show or disprove what your mouth says.

In Neuro-Linguistic Programming (NLP), carried out techniques are strengthened thru non-verbal verbal exchange. That technique you could manage the emotions of a person just via the usage of appropriate body movements and gestures that add conviction on your statements. Unlike in public talking, even though, the movements you may use are instead restricted.

If you doubt the energy of body gestures, attempt those easy actions and watch how people can be hypnotized through the use of way of you.

When in a crowd or with a fixed of buddies, difficulty your finger to the sky and appearance up.

Or yawn.

See how many will look at your gesture.

Powerful, is not it?

Here are the body actions and gestures that you need to keep in mind every time attending an interview.

1. Leaning ahead

Leaning in advance indicates your motive to pay hobby attentively and speak overtly. To an interviewer, it could advise:

• "I am keen to pass this interview."

• "I want you to recognize me better."

• "Tell me greater approximately your organization."

• "You are in reality searching on the first-rate individual you could want for the manner."

Welcoming the interviewer is the first-class manner to get his hobby and look at his reactions carefully. A caution, even though: leaning an excessive amount of is visible as an invasion of private area. Make outstanding that there can be enough space among you, lest you'll be accused of going too intimate.

2. Touching the pulse while shaking arms

When you shake hands (by no means neglect this earlier than the interview), barely expand your index and center finger clearly enough to touch the interviewer's pulse. Doing that is said to push the relationship a hint greater non-public but not too familiar. It enables in showing your sincerity and honesty.

However, be perceptive of man or woman in advance than doing it, specially if the interviewer belongs to the alternative sex. It might be misinterpreted as a gesture tainted with sexual connotation.

3. Opening your palm on the equal time as speakme

Expressing your critiques and thoughts matched with hand gestures upload emphasis and conviction. Opening your palm shows which you are definitely expressing your mind and no longer forcing your mind to the interview. It is also just like pronouncing which you are open to arguments.

On the alternative hand, speakme while maintaining a stiff, motionless posture indicates that you are not too confident with what you're pronouncing; or worse, the whole thing you say is scripted.

Clenching the fist works actually high-quality in public speaking, however keep away from doing it in interviews as it implies sturdy feelings which may be beside the factor in an interview putting (you are being interviewed, now not attempted).

four. Maintain eye touch

You in reality recognize how important eye contact is thru now, however it isn't enough to test the interviewer on the same time due to the fact the communique is going on. Look right away into his eyes and lock it. It says loads about your self belief, sincerity, honesty and credibility.

You can damage your contact, but only at the identical time as you are talking and not in advance than. It is a way to offer the interviewer a respiration space (looking at every other for numerous minutes can come to be awkward in the long run). However, if you may ruin the touch earlier than developing a announcement, it'd mean that you are making up recollections (see financial ruin 7).

five. Nodding

This smooth gesture speaks certainly of your interest. You want to make the interviewer experience that he's being listened to, understood and believed. Cocking your head every time you listen some component new or exciting moreover boosts the ego of the interviewer.

Aside from the recommended frame moves and gestures, you need to also maintain in thoughts a few taboos in an interview.

1. Crossing the palms

You should by no means drift your hands. This is a greater intimate gesture among those who understand a manner to take care of each different that asserts "I will concentrate to you, but we would have an difficulty about this."

If the interviewer crosses his or her arms, it isn't always a fantastic sign and you want to find out techniques to interrupt that pattern. One technique is to draw some thing on a bit of paper on the identical time as speaking or display a few information out of your record. This will make him lean in advance and optimistically uncross his hands.

2. Frowning

It says not anything extremely good. It is a robust gesture to expose opposition and unhappiness.

3. Pouting the lips

This is an casual gesture that pronounces "I am no longer fantastic approximately that." It is normally considered inoffensive however best in case you have already got an affable courting with the person.

4. Leaning backwards

It both method you're dropping interest or turning into overconfident. Either way, it hurts your probabilities of having the approval.

five. Sitting better

Some people would probable say that it's far notable as it magnifies authority and effect. However, do bear in mind that an interviewer won't want someone who acts bossy or overpowering for the duration of the primary meeting. You are looking to get his approval, now not sell a car thru emotional manipulation. If you located your chair is in reality too excessive for the interviewer, modify it (if possible), just so you will be at the identical diploma as him.

Chapter 4: Matching Connections with NLP

Neuro-Linguistic Programming (NLP) emerge as first systematized within the Seventies to aid in the analyzing of people who've a tough time with language acquisition. Through the years, the special NLP techniques have advanced and had practical makes use of in the marketplace, public talking or even interviews. By the use of it collectively with entire aura and right gestures and frame language, you may without problems and powerfully effect the feelings of some special individual subconsciously.

Mirroring

Mirroring attracts human beings collectively, giving them that immediate connection important to earn maintain in thoughts. It presentations the similar values humans share and with the aid of way of NLP, it may be used to strongly have an effect on a person.

Mirroring is completed in severa strategies but for interview periods, I even have listed 5 primary techniques.

First is thru matching enthusiasm and electricity. When you communicate with an interviewer that oozes with enthusiasm, now not reciprocating might also indicate disinterest or insensitivity. All you need to do is in shape the opportunity person's strength, so that you right away have a common denominator.

Second is with the aid of matching key terms and key phrases, moreover known as mirror phrases. Matching key phrases and key terms offer continuity to the go with the flow of conversation, indicating that your degree of interest fits that of the interviewer.

For instance, the interviewer asks you "How should you operate your strengths in unleashing your full capacity in the route of the improvement of the business organization?" You can respond by using saying "I can unleash my whole functionality for the advantage of the organisation by means of the use of the use of utilising my strengths and improving on them..." It in a few manner lowers the interviewer's impact of your responsiveness if you can veer from the crucial factor terms he uses. Remember that interviewers are commonly seeking out keywords that in shape theirs.

Another model is to copy the remaining four or five phrases that had been utilized by the interviewer. Repeat the same terms, then begin your sentence at the same time as replying.

Third is with the aid of the use of matching body moves and gestures. This have to by no means be completed excessively as it can without issue look mocking; however while used the proper manner, it could realign your non-verbal communique to that of the interviewer's.

For example, if the interviewer leans earlier while asking a question, it is a signal that he's putting sufficient emphasis to its significance in judging you. Match his motion thru the usage of additionally leaning beforehand.

Fourth is thru tone matching. Tone is associated with enthusiasm. Tone matching is clearly a unconscious flattery as it suggests respect and admiration. It is also essential to check the speaking fashion of the interviewer, so that you can fit it as well. It will seem awkward for the interviewer in case you live very formal at the same time as he's already the usage of a conversational tone. Clearly, you aren't getting the message that it is ok to loosen up a chunk and in reality be herbal. That loss of sensitivity is a mark down for you.

The fifth method can be a bit hard for a number of you. It is to breath on the equal way.

Look at the chest area and nostril and be aware if you could wholesome the identical rise and fall. This is a completely effective approach to track in to the identical frequency of considering every other individual.

If you aren't able to draw near this fifth technique, don't worry too much as this is greater for the intermediate NLP men.If you can, it is a bonus.

Mirroring need to in no manner be incorrect for mimicking, which is commonly taken into consideration rude, sarcastic and in a few unspecified time in the destiny, insulting. If there are a whole lot of hints taking place from the interviewer, do now not try to reflect the whole thing exactly as they take place because it will make the mirroring appearance planned and mocking.

Do not change your sitting role each time the interviewer modifications feature. Do now not begin all of your sentences with all the key phrases that the interviewer simply said. It is likewise deemed inappropriate to healthy pitch, in particular if it manifestly is not your herbal pitch.

Reverse Psychology

Well, there's a sixth method that is form of 'semi-mirroring". Worth to say as there can be a sturdy opportunity that you want to apply it in your interview.

Read on...

Using opposite psychology in disagreeing and rejecting opinions is the tremendous manner to remain respectful but corporation together collectively together with your very very own beliefs and ideas. Instead of the use of "I beg to disagree" or "I certainly have a awesome opinion on that", say "I admire that" or "I be given that factor of view" followed thru and, no longer however. Or better but, begin a ultra-current sentence.

Chapter 5: How to Build Rapport with the Interviewer

Rapport is described as "a dating marked through concord, conformity, accord or affinity." An interviewer and interviewee should meet on the identical net web page to create this type of connection, but that is almost impossible in case you are groping for the melody to harmonize and the same old to conform.

It is tough to construct a rapport with an interviewer in case you do no longer meet eye to eye. Unfortunately, doing so includes information his goals, preferences and person – matters that are not exactly clean to understand on the number one assembly.

One manner to bridge this hole is with the beneficial useful resource of putting your self inside the footwear of the interviewer, thinking like him and knowledge what he is searching out in an interviewee, whether or no longer it's far for a mission software program, school admission or everyday records accumulating.

Every interviewer has his very very own set of requirements, regardless if he surely likes what he's doing or not (i.E. He might rent an applicant that doesn't fit his personal preference, however absolutely meet the qualifications of the agency employer). Those requirements meet his intention and if you meet them, you already surpass severa tiers of the connection approach.

You need to conform with the standards to bring together a rapport. What are the commonplace criteria of interviewers that you have to understand?

Substance

Some humans speak, however although do now not say some thing at the identical time as some say lots without speaking an excessive amount of. The distinction is substance.

When human beings try and please interviewers an excessive amount of, they wear a spurious man or woman and come to be really awkward to talk with. They normally tend to crack half of-hearted jokes that fall flat and say spur-of-the-second quips which can be not regularly concept of. The humor they're looking to inject into the verbal exchange and their willingness to expose that they can be exciting can absolutely get the interviewer's hobby. However, most of the time, this form of method that lacks substance does now not skip past the "hobby degree."

A professional essayist will make his element clear proper on the introduction on the identical time as an newbie will beat all through the bush and try to provoke with highfalutin words that might be interesting however do no longer surely make a problem or stance.

The equal is authentic with character. You must offer substance first earlier than you try to seem thrilling and amusing to talk with. Substance nonetheless bears more weight than persona because of the fact in an agency, substance is urgently needed on the equal time as persona may be labored on over the years.

Packaging

This criterion is defined as "enchantment upon first look" – the first effect you leave to human beings based totally to your look and movements. Do you appearance (and scent) neat? Do you appearance professional? Do you appearance a person who can be relied on regardless of the truth that strangers stroll together with you in a dark alley? You can in no manner discover that magic connection if human beings repel you right away upon first glance.

Almost all interviews associated with utility are deemed formal even in a casual setting. That way you are expected to appearance your exceptional regardless of the reality that the enterprise organization you're the usage of to does no longer in reality have a strict get dressed code. A huge mistake a few human beings dedicate is sticking with their quirky and comparatively unusual style with the reason that the authenticity in their character can only be tested through their actual fashion (and hygiene) taste. However, they neglect that once they may be seeking to get into an business enterprise, they may be those to make the vital changes.

Go to an interview like you're selling yourself, and not showing your body in a few shape of an summary museum.

Responsiveness

Communication is given massive significance everywhere. All your exquisite mind and awesome competency are useless if no different people can recognize you because of terrible communique. That is first manifested in an interview through your responsiveness. Interestingly, your interest, hobby to element and exuberance also are gauged by using the use of the use of your responsiveness. You absolutely do not anticipate to make a connection even as the opposite line does now not deliver any response.

So how are you judged collectively along with your responsiveness?

First is by the use of quickness. Do you respond speedy and as accurate as viable? Interviewers are required to illustrate staying electricity; however obviously, additionally they have got a limit. Can you don't forget what number of interviews they should do in a unmarried day? Do them a select by manner of being honest, as loads as you can.

Second is via way of sensitivity. Do you believe you studied before you communicate? Do you recognize the manner to maintain reviews that do not offer any benefit besides? Do you recognize what it way to offend verbally? If you have got got tactfulness for your body, convey it all inside the interview because of the fact it could make the distinction amongst approval and rejection.

Third is with the aid of brevity. Do that during a mean interview, the interviewer speaks more than the interviewee? Conciseness and eloquence show sophistication and for an interviewer, the ones are a prime switch on. Brevity in reality means that responding with substance can never get replaced with the resource of any large vocabulary.

Fourth is with the resource of your straightforwardness. The decisiveness of an employee is given extra elements. He is aware of what he needs to do and what desires to appear. He can supply smooth and accurate solutions when asked. Most importantly, he does not keep away from essential questions.

Last is with the useful resource of clarity. Can you accept as true with that a mean very last pastime interview lasts for forty minutes? For technical positions, it lasts for up to two hours. Nothing can be extra traumatic than talking to a person who says not some thing but obscurity for added than half of of an hour. It effects in a useless verbal exchange that does not justify all of your claims.

Practice your answers to FAQs, so you can choose out your phrases properly. It is higher in case your word selections will in form those of the enterprise like their vision, challenge, tagline or motto. Preparing days in advance than an interview will allow you to slender down your solutions to FAQs to steer them to shorter but as clean as viable.

Experience

Relevant experience will certainly remember towards your approval and admission, however what if you do now not have a whole lot to provide in terms of this department inside the first vicinity? It is probably very hard to construct a rapport with a person who appears some element one in every of a type from what you want to offer.

If you apprehend that you have the downside with regards to experience, display instances even as you exhibited an eagerness to study and adapt to the requirements, like in case you studied a cutting-edge-day pc software application just to get a assignment executed or in case you observed out a present day language sincerely to make certain that your new customer is assisted to the fantastic of your expertise and potential.

As in opposition to what some humans assume, enthusiasm isn't always examined with facial features or tone of voice. You can sound excited and glad but nevertheless lack drive to show your enthusiasm. It is tested with the aid of manner of movement which you have taken inside the past, so put together to justify it.

It is straightforward to say that you are eager to analyze or is prepared for the annoying conditions, but it's miles hard to again up your claims with actual picks, movements and outcomes which you have met within the beyond.

Preparedness

With the internet almost presenting you the whole lot you want to recognize about the employer or man or woman you want to speak to, there's now not any exceptional excuse no longer to come to an interview absolutely organized. Seeing query marks during your face upon stepping into the venue right now repels the interviewer. It technique that your determination is inclined. Nobody desires to soak up someone who is only there halfheartedly.

If you're severe approximately constructing a rapport, you have to improve the appeal you exude through your not unusual packaging with preparedness – preparedness that want to reflect on your manner of speaking.

First, do a studies approximately the profile and historical past of the employer you're making plans to enroll in. What is it all about? What exactly is its feature? You need to understand what you have become your self into, so you won't be stuck by the usage of wonder at the same time as the interviewer tells you his/her expectancies.

Their imaginative and prescient and undertaking must additionally be aligned alongside side your goals and plans due to the fact they want a person who can assist them to the top. Plans without intention alignment do no longer make any connection in any respect. Most records is available on respectable net web sites and social media account. Or better but, ask the individual that scheduled your interview for facts like who may be interviewing you, for what, mainly, how prolonged will it is and what necessities they will have.

Chapter 6: Avoiding False Connection

While body gestures are effective, it is able to be a double component sword.

In NLP, language or the selection of terms is a subject by using the use of itself. For instance, " I can not manipulate to pay for it" and "How can I certainly have sufficient cash it?" has exceptional motives of motion. The former is disempowering at the same time as the latter is empowering.

In this segment, the frame language and verbal language which provide a false interpretation are provided.

This is what existence coaches name false connection. This is the time even as most effective one side, maximum possibly the interviewee, feels that there can be a connection occurring. In truth, it's far an insignificant miscommunication because many interviewees will be inclined to take what interviewers say at face fee.

False connection may be a profession killer because it breaks the momentum by means of making an interviewee each enjoy overconfident and too complacent, or experience defeated and rejected. What started out out out right may appear wrong ultimately if someone being interviewed turns into too cushty, too familiar or too pessimistic.

Not everything an interviewer says is in reality meant. Some are recurring statements that every one professional interviewers come to say to offer oblique answers and warning signs and signs.

Perhaps, it's also a way of pronouncing "I'm sorry, I sincerely such as you but our manager ordered us no longer to provide away tips of viable effects." Or "You appear truly amazing, however sadly, your qualifications do no longer match our necessities."

Do now not fall for false connection. Avoid giving colors to common interview statements that might spoil your possibilities of having the slot.

1. "You are truly certified for this undertaking."

Being licensed does no longer recommend you may get the system. There is a opportunity that every one candidates are certified; it is simplest a remember of identifying who qualifies terrific. Sometimes, it is the little nuances that make the distinction. Perhaps, it's miles a massive smile, a warmth handshake, an lovable fragrance or a fixed of pearly white tooth. Do no longer permit the compliment to straight away go to your head as it could disrupt your reputation.

2. "You are promising."

As cited inner the earlier bankruptcy, there are instances even as the functionality of an interviewee may be the critical clincher. Your capability to analyze, re-analyze and develop can take you an prolonged, long manner in something vicinity; however what if distinct interviewees do now not best display capability however actual, usable traits which may be geared up for deployment?

Most of the time, this announcement does not have any which means the least bit, so do not slacken off certainly but. You will lose your aura the immediately the interviewer feels you are overconfident.

3. "We will keep your document for opportunities that could match your qualifications."

This is the aspect in which many interviewees start to appear defeated and lose all of the enthusiasm they delivered in the interview. The interviewer would possibly expect that every one the passion the interviewee indicates at the start of the interview is all just for display.

The connotation of this statement virtually method "We are not hiring you, however we're capable of don't forget your resume for future venture openings." However, that isn't usually right so something top notch start you have, surely flow into and maintain it.

When an HR tells you this, in reality preserve going. Give the entirety you've were given due to the fact the curtain is but to shut. The interviewer is absolutely doing what is legally predicted of him, that is to maintain all files of applicants whether or no longer employed or rejected.

4. "I'm glad you purchased right here nowadays (even on a brief be aware)."

Some humans would possibly read this as "You are the most critical candidate we've got." Do not take a look at something into it because of the reality your ego-boosting knowledge may moreover spoil your risk of really connecting with the interviewer. Remember that humility creates magical connection.

This announcement is without a doubt mechanically utilized by interviewers to house you and say "thank you" for certainly taking the time to use. It does not endorse a few factor.

five. "You are actually a huge assist."

People regularly pay interest this on every occasion they're interviewed for statistics or opinion. The interviewer is sincerely sharing his gratitude without absolutely which means that it all of the time. It can be a large ego-booster, too large that it makes people neglect about about to self-investigate and validate whether or no longer or now not they have definitely emerge as useful or no longer.

Ask yourself first if you have truly furnished a few element huge to the interviewer. If no longer, deliver a letter of apology (or message) for now not being a splendid help, or famend which you have given insufficient help and truely promise to assist however viable. Acknowledging leaves a extraordinary impact, a prerequisite to actual connection.

Like statements, gestures can also reason fake connections. Some human beings misinterpret gestures and body actions of interviewers to be symptoms of reputation of their person, evaluations and developments even as in reality, those non-verbal communications are truly symptoms and signs of acknowledgement. This clean misinterpretation can lead human beings to act too acquainted, too pleasant or too self-targeted which is probably usually visible as no longer some element but essential turn-off.

1. A heat smile

Because maximum people see interviews as terrifying, furthermore they expect stern interviewers who lack pleasance and accommodativeness. So once they meet a pleasing character whole with a extensive, heat smile at the back of the desk, they have a tendency to take into account that they have got have already got been given a further element ("Maybe my resume is sincerely too sudden" or "Maybe I am too appealing").

A smile isn't whatever however a pleasing gesture. Most of the time, it does not say some element about your possibilities of having a vote. However, that is most probable a sign which you are being welcomed to construct a connection, and that the interviewer is genuinely geared up how you'll do that.

2. Nodding

Throughout the interview, it's miles very likely that the interviewer will nod whether or not he consents with what you're pronouncing or not. Some humans push similarly with their lies within the notion that the interviewer believes what they're pronouncing. Unlike in a ordinary communique, nodding in an interview approach "I am listening to you" and now not something extra. An interview is all approximately you and not about addressing a controversy or confronting you for telling lies. That is the scary part of it; it's far tough to look if an interviewer has no longer something however disagreement with you.

Do not run the bigotry to your head while you notice an interviewer nods from the begin until the cease. Just focus on staying right and humble in choice to giving egotistic perspectives and reviews.

Chapter 7: How to Read an Interviewer

A magic connection amongst you and the interviewer is a certain way to win his/her coronary coronary coronary heart, or instead, vote; but, it is with the aid of hook or via manner of criminal difficult to do, specifically if you have no concept what is going on within the interviewer's mind, and what is being anticipated of you. Unfortunately, interviewers now not regularly display their requirements and private desire in an interviewee. How will you pierce thru the interviewer's estimating glances with a deadpan face?

Know what maximum interviewers are wondering within the path of an interview; this is the extremely good way to fulfill along with her or him eye to eye. From there, you could start constructing rapport and get hold of as genuine with all to your benefit. This can be a great deal less of an trouble if you are being interviewed for a characteristic or facts, however it could be the whole thing if you are the only trying the preference which includes in a activity or university interview.

Remember that interviews are specially mind video video games. Interviewers will try to play with you until you mistakenly deliver away your real individual, actual intentions, and real charge without any pretensions, revealing your weaknesses in the long run. They will do the whole lot to interrupt down the wall that separates yourself perception and insecurities. Nonetheless, you may discover a steady way spherical that with the aid of manner of the usage of searching beforehand to their strategies and gambling alongside aspect them without going spurious.

1. They right away judge you through your look

Here is a reality which you want to take: skills, mindset and information may be superior over the years with experience and right training, while the physical look can not.

Many massive agencies with thorough worker training packages and business enterprise-licensed training modules care much less approximately your modern-day competency reputation due to the truth what is maximum crucial for them is your capability to enhance and observe (have a look at: capability). These organizations spend an entire lot of coins at the high-quality strolling shoes to make the greater excessive candidate the outstanding. However, similarly they take into consideration the fact that no instructor may want to make a person appearance attractive or extraordinary searching regardless of makeovers.

Yes, there are corporations that prioritize accurate appears over competency.

It might possibly seem shallow; however positive, interviewers do determine you through appearance. Good have an effect on via physical look might be very vital, mainly for jobs that require face-to-face interplay with customers like within the case of salesmen, real assets marketers and waiters.

2. You are boring and looks stupid

Sometimes, an interview takes vicinity for the sake of getting it completed like while any character dreams precise facts from you. That does now not advocate the interviewer is likewise inquisitive about what is taking location, however if you need to establish long lasting dating with him, you'll choose some recommendations that display his proper reviews.

If you are too keen to speak up and solution organized questions, you should also, at the least, have the keenness to pay attention and be receptive of the interviewer's diffused reactions to have a successful communication.

Are you dominating the conversation an excessive amount of that the opportunity character not sees any necessity to chime in? It might be due to the fact the interviewer thinks which you are too entire of yourself that it is already useless to try and start a actual, wholesome discourse. Obviously, that creates a horrible influence.

Repeatedly pronouncing matters that the interviewer already is aware about moreover positioned you vulnerable to being perceived as dull. Do now not harp on flattering the agency or the interviewer specially if it's miles an apparent reality. Stating what's already indicated on your resume additionally does now not make any difference; in reality, it'd appear offending for a few due to the reality it is like announcing that the interviewer does not understand a manner to interpret what he reads.

Maybe you are saying topics that do not healthy their necessities. This typically happens whilst an interviewee fails to do his homework and study the commercial enterprise enterprise and the position he's applying for.

What you have to do is to slow down, allow him do his mission, and take a look at in which you are likely getting it wrong. Look for hints.

An interviewer who does not set up eye contact is announcing he isn't always inquisitive about you. His mind is probably lagging a few other place, probable questioning "this is vain" or "I want it ends quickly."

The brilliant way to get his interest again is to say some thing unexpected for as long as you apprehend it's far inside your limits. For example, if recounting your revel in at art work does no longer seem to pique his hobby, draw out your exquisite card and make a big declare in conjunction with announcing that you'll double their profits in 12 months, otherwise you see reasons to revise their considerable jogging techniques.

If you word that the interviewer's lips are twitching, you need to moreover be hearing him say "Really now?" It implies that he thinks you're exaggerating, so proper away once more up your declare with achievements or successes you had in the beyond.

For example, in case you say you can be their pinnacle income agent in 365 days, you need to nation similar achievements to expose that you could honestly do it. If you may claim which you are able to turning into an imperative worker, u . S . Some proofs like how you have have been given been provided a boost in your previous venture only for them to keep you.

Raising eyebrow furthermore creates a massive assertion, indicating that the interview does no longer take delivery of as real with what you're pronouncing. Upon getting the hint, reconsider your statements if you stated a few thing that does not observe their requirements or standards. If you're confident that what you've got virtually stated is suitable, attention on defensive it with legitimate elements without sounding accountable of committing a mistake.

There is not any need to normally get the interviewer to agree with you due to the truth businesses need a person who ought to make his private alternatives. Just make sure you realize the way to shield your selections and be consistent at the aspect of your guiding thoughts.

3. They are inclined to make a gap even if there is none in reality to house promising candidates

A agenda for interview is not regularly cancelled however the truth that they have already visible someone they want to hire. They will though accommodate every body who has been scheduled because of the truth they'll be legally required to. However, that does not imply that it's far the give up of the street for you.

When an interviewer tells you that they have already employed a person (or the individual interviewed earlier than you), do now not display any signal of defeat and as an alternative, certainly do what you want to do and show that they have got been given it all incorrect. Even if it is actual that a slot isn't always to be had, they will be despite the fact that inclined to make one should you be capable of get the interviewer's be given as proper with.

If they can not truely make an opening, there is constantly the risk that a latest feature will open up rapid, and that you may be the immediately alternative. There is also the possibility that the simplest they employed acquired't take delivery of the offer besides.

Once you begin an interview, do no longer flip another time. Just positioned your eyes on the target and maintain pushing hard for it.

four. They look for your eyes for guidelines of mendacity

The left difficulty of the thoughts is the most effective in-fee for creativity. In psychology, those who regularly go with the waft their eyes to the left even as talking are said to be mendacity or making up recollections. It is not an correct declare, especially for folks which can be obviously willing to their modern aspect (e.G. Applicants for writing and designing positions); but due to the truth most HR staffs honestly have a historical past in psychology, doing it might deliver them a wrong interpretation (in particular if they will be already disagreeing or questioning your statements).

Likewise, keep away from moving closer to your proper because it is also visible as a signal of mendacity (the mind and frame are contralateral, because of this that that after the left facet of the mind is active, the right thing of the body is greater energetic).

To stay constant, just keep your eye touch or if you have to interrupt, appearance to the proper or down (looking up is as proper as displaying a clean thoughts).

Even if you can't observe an interviewer well, the great information is that you could have an impact on her or him if you may draw close your frame language, decorate your air of mystery and assemble higher rapport.

Chapter 8: The Interview Mindset

This bankruptcy will characteristic the inspiration upon which the subsequent chapters are built. While most books devote loads of pages to the practical tips within the previous few chapters, they'll serve no reason if now not found with the interview attitude.

Why is the interview thoughts-set so critical? Simply because of the truth we stay out who we consider we're. We act out our self-given identification. And if you don't see your self because the most capable person that need to be hired, there can be no way you could act the issue.

So what's the interview thoughts-set? It is in reality the attitude that seeks nothing from human beings and best for humans.

Let me offer an reason in the back of.

It is exceptional on the same time as you don't are in search of a few aspect from human beings, be it their hobby, their adoration, their popularity. It's exquisite while you don't want on the way to you actually have a danger of earning it. People are repelled with the useful resource of manner of neediness, possibly because of the reality they see themselves in it. But after they come across someone who is assured, stable, and now not looking of humans's adoration, humans begin to notice.

And then to seal the deal, at the same time as this confident person isn't always fine self-enough, however seeks the fine of others, people can't assist but be drawn in. Why? Because this is counterintuitive. It's no longer regular. But while you discover ways to hold close this mind-set, you learn how to win people.

The reality is, human beings like, keep in mind, hire, and observe human beings that:

1.   They like and recognize

2.   Like and are inquisitive about them

three.   Are just like them

We're going to interrupt this thoughts-set into five concepts or the five pillars that create this attitude.

It is important that you expand the ones intellectual conduct time past regulation to grasp lifestyles's interviews.

Principle #1: Be the Leader

Be the chief. Even at the identical time as you're now not. Display authority, even whilst you don't have it. The fact is, you don't want an real function of management to present off a experience of have an effect on. Not in any respect. Leadership occurs even as you come upon as someone who is privy to what she or he's doing. Somebody with a longtime revel in of self and purpose.

In the interview room, this seems like you displaying self guarantee in yourself. It manner taking walks into the interview with the thoughts-set that some time is limited and treasured, you have got got excellent options (or may have them),   that this enterprise agency desperately wants to fill this characteristic, and also you'll offer them a while to promote it to you.

What you input the room with that thoughts-set, your responses and your mind-set will usually trade. It may be definitely unique than on foot into the room, hands-crossed, arms sweaty, hoping they'll together with you and your resume out of the alternative 2 hundred applicants.

No.

The first step is to inform your self which you do no longer need this hobby. You'll discover different jobs. You'll discover superb strategies. But your life does no longer depend upon this mission, this interview, or this hiring supervisor. You refuse to provide them that strength over you.

A CEO or army cutting-edge will by no means walk right proper into a conference room, hoping the verbal exchange will bypass nicely and people will like them. They have too many precise subjects to care approximately and their time is constrained. Their existence, safety, popularity, or self confidence really isn't be threatened by using manner of manner of absolutely everyone in that room and all and sundry is aware of that when they stroll in.

At this component you can argue: But they have already got a project. They already have admire. They are already in that role of manage so of course it's clean for them.

And that's in which you're wrong. Because a fulfillment CEO's, generals, and leaders all had this mind-set extended earlier than they ever have been given their position. In truth, it modified into this very thoughts-set that were given them there.

All this to say which you have to wake up every morning with a smooth enjoy of who you're and what your motive is. If you don't understand what it's far, then find it. Write it out on paper. You need to recognize your undertaking on this global and your precise contribution that only YOU can offer. Not Bill Gates, now not Steve Jobs, not your hiring supervisor, no longer your next-door neighbor, however you. What talent, individual trait, capabilities, or revel in that you uniquely have that devices you apart.

And then ask your self this question: With my specialty, what distinction in this world am I called to make?

It can be which you have a keen eye for imagining designs and mind that have not began to be created, that the arena wishes.

It might be that you're a superb organizer and you're referred to as to steer agencies of people to new endeavors.

Whatever it's far, don't do some thing until you solution this query.

When you solution this query and deliver your life to it, control starts offevolved. When you have embraced this mind-set, you'll have the capability to walk into any room as a frontrunner with a described challenge and defined private values. A undertaking and values that you take delivery of as proper with with complete conviction are vital and useful for this worldwide and for without a doubt anybody in it. That consists of your hiring supervisor, at the same time as you stroll in for your interview.

And at the same time as you've definitely embraced this imaginative and prescient of your self and of your lifestyles, you'll begin to emerge as any character who doesn't need whatever from others, in any respect. And that's the start of management.

"The question isn't who is going to allow me; it's who is going to prevent me." Ayn Rand.

Principle #2: Be Knowledgeable

"Ipsa Scientia Potestas Est

Knowledge itself is power."

Sir Francis Francis William Maxwell Aitken

To be a real chief and real master of interviews and lifestyles, you should be informed. There isn't always any manner spherical this. You want to commit your self to a lifelong quest of mastering and growing to your understanding.

You can tell at once who the chief inside the room is thru seeing who every body definitely turns to whilst a query is asked. Even in the event that they don't have the decent position of authority. Why? Because they're the maximum possibly to apprehend the answer. And folks that recognize are those we observe.

Every wonderful leader in history has been a reader of books, journals, magazines, and nowadays, blogs and internet articles. It is handiest thru a cultivated addiction of mastering that you begin to get a maintain close on how everything connects on this worldwide, from economics, to political generation, to inventory market, to human psychology, biology, and even chemistry.

This isn't to say which you want to be an professional on each state of affairs. That is probably not possible and a futile venture. Yet to at the least have a framework on the ones extraordinary arenas and sectors of existence and society is to provide you get right of entry to to the top 10% of those who stand out above the organization. The 10% of mother and father that are probably to be followed.

There is a motive for this.

The sad fact is really too frequently our educational systems are wrong in that we're recommended to pursue instructors over education. We are rewarded for our check-taking abilities, as opposed to our skills of creativity and success.

Most of society is skilled to stay via the device and to try for the matters the machine encourages: Get immediately A's, look at for lengthy hours to bypass checks (even in case you don't hold close the fabric), partake in sports most effective to buff up your resume, visit college and get a degree, examine for the sake of reading and passing, get an internship role or , and then start using for jobs.

Hopefully you land a task and you may settle into a comfortable existence.

This creates a societal tunnel-vision. We have sacrificed training for systematic teachers which may be simplest rewarded if we look at the tool and sample that has been laid out for us.

This shape of gaining knowledge of does now not create leaders.

True leaders bypass past that, whether or no longer deliberately or with the aid of the usage of twist of fate, and are looking for to find out how the arena works. They are looking for to find out how human beings paintings and the way way of life works.

This takes place thru education, not teachers. This takes location via non-public observe pushed through manner of the usage of passion, no longer punishment. This is inspired thru using hobby, no longer curriculums.

And in case you extend and draw close this addiction of continuously learning now not for the sake of grades, but for the sake of boom, then you could have a break via. Not many humans make it via this. Too many are content cloth with gambling the educational sport, doing a little issue it takes to get proper grades, to get appropriate resumes, to get mediocre jobs, and post themselves to regardless of the gadget, hiring managers, and corporations need from them, for the rest in their lives.

You need to ruin free from this.

It is on the equal time as you increase this addiction, you may be a leader and be any character well really worth following. You will are seeking out to create, not in reality to conform. You may be described with the resource of a ardour to sail the seas, in preference to the fear of rocking the proverbial boat.

When you draw close those ideas we've stated to this point, you will become a person that human beings esteem; that people like; that people respect. That is the first step to govern and this is the first step to the interview attitude.

Principle #3: Be an Expert Affirmer

The natural disposition of someone is to live a self-absorbed life. It's a unhappy truth, but as I referred to in the first few pages of this ebook, that's how I lived.

As human beings, we're all sincerely self-targeted and overly self-conscious. Call it psychology, or evolutionary developments, or sin, or something worldview you return from, we can not deny this truth. But we are able to use it to our gain.

Remember, the 3 sorts of people that humans like?

1.   People that they prefer

2.   People that like them

three.   People which might be like them.

The first requirements (be a leader and be understanding) set you up to be the primary shape of character. People like leaders. People have a study folks who are not needy or depending on others. And people recognize the ones which can be informed.

To be the second form of man or woman is the goal of this principle.

If you want any man or woman to like you and agree with you, you must be their largest affirmer. You need to be their biggest fan. You must display off actual hobby in their life, their interests, their passions, their struggles, and their fears. You want to authentically need to understand extra approximately them and they'll comprehend if you are actual or not.

And the most effective manner to absolutely show border-line obsessive interest in every person is to be someone that does not want some element from them. In distinct phrases: get over your self. You in truth can not be sincerely interested by their life if you are desperately dependant and in need of their approval or confirmation.

You must resolve firmly that you do NOT need this man or woman to like you, whether or now not or no longer it's a woman or boy you're romantically interested in, or if it's a hiring supervisor, or a modern day classmate. You need to find this feel of self-approval a few other place. You must be self-secured to your non-public enjoy of self-worth, for your values, and on your specific undertaking.

Then, and handiest then, are you able to dedicate your self to being interested in super people. And take delivery of as real with me, the ones sort of humans are unusual. But I'm wonderful you apprehend that.

Let's supply this lower back to the interview room.

If you walk in to the interview room, no longer worried about getting this gadget because you don't need this interest. Not wringing your hands, nervously hoping you'll be favored. Instead, if you walk in, confident to your cause, with the mindset which you are giving them the possibility to hire you, you are freed to behave obviously. You can be extra cushty and be an professional affirmer. Your technique now's to do your satisfactory to obviously affirm anything you may approximately them, making them experience precious and preferred. They will don't forget this.

Whenever you have got were given conversations with new people, who're the humans you do not forget to at the prevailing time? People that complimented you. People that stated high-quality things about you and affirmed you. Even if it become as clean as them pronouncing they preferred your shoes or your blouse. Do you consider the way you right now felt about the ones people? You preferred them.

If you had been a hiring supervisor, undertaking masses of interviews with masses of humans a day, who ought to you keep in mind? Those that made you experience affirmed and unique.

You can touch upon the way you need their shirt, or if the concern arises, you may casually start a conversation approximately their hobbies or their existence. Only humans with this proper thoughts-set can ever need to carry out this absolutely, and it's those people that get employed to come to be leaders.

Principle #4: Get in Their World

This precept gives with the remaining form of character that people like: People which might be like them. If you've ever been a new place, whether travelling, or a present day school, or a trendy project, who do you gravitate in the course of?

People which can be which consist of you.

It can be some issue from how they get dressed, their ethnicity, their man or woman, and masses of others. And on the identical time as you start to get to understand human beings greater, you're drawn even inside the direction of individuals who share comparable pursuits as you, whether or now not interests, or faith, or beyond reviews.

Those with the interview attitude realize this nicely and could do the whole thing to make the ones connections. When those connections are made, hiring managers are 50% much more likely to don't forget your call.

Obviously you're going to want to do this glaringly. In exceptional phrases, this does not name for an ungainly, "Hi I'm Henry, WHAT DO YOU LIKE TO DO?" Experts at this try to clearly thread this right right right into a verbal exchange.

"You've got an exciting remaining call. May I ask wherein it's from?"

And considering every body loves taking approximately themselves, they'll solution. At this factor, you can say:

"Oh, it's French? I went to France 2 years within the past, it changed into lovely!"

Or if you didn't visit France,

"Oh that's adorable! I actually have a friend from France and she or he's commonly raving about _____."

If you're lucky, this may spark further communication. You may not be able to make connections with out issues, however that is a capacity you need to increase. You need to train your eyes to look for subjects that might create conversations.

What does their espresso mug say?

What does their University Diploma say? What did they examine?

What does their tattoo suggest?

If you may set up a connection with them (or really anybody in existence), this can located you in a remarkable league all together. You'll understand that this skills may be proper now accelerated with the useful aid of the way professional you are in principle 2.

Principle #five: Be Reserved

This fifth and final principle should probable seem a chunk out of vicinity, however there may be a fantastic reason for this element of this thoughts-set. Bluntly said, humans admire folks that never show all of their cards. I don't suggest in a shady, suspicious type of way inflicting humans to question whether or not or no longer or now not you're a murderer.

Rather, I mean to signify to behave in this type of way that you continuously have things beneath control, even at the same time as you don't. Always appear to have an opportunity plan, for the sake of others. Why? Because human beings look to leaders who have solutions, even though the leaders don't have answer.

This is a not unusual human characteristic and it's regularly exhibited inside the films we watch. All of the leaders which are portrayed as professional are also portrayed as barely mysterious and reserved, as even though they typically recognize some thing we don't and we are able to take delivery of as real with them for that. Just some examples of this are Dumbledore, Professor Xavier, Yoda, Batman, Jack Sparrow, Jesus, Rick Grimes (Walking Dead), Oliver Queen (Arrow). We can skip on all the time.

Take be aware that it's not that we're borrowing from the movies and delusion. Instead, it's the reserve. The movies without a doubt portray the tendencies of human nature. We look as an lousy lot as leaders that appear to continuously apprehend what they're doing and are reserved and humble about it.

Chapter 9: Practical Tips for Preparation

Now that we've mentioned the interview thoughts-set (which, like numerous behavior, will not shape in a single day), we will maintain to the lesser critical tips. These hints are useful, however best if completed from the right attitude. Nonetheless, we will find out them.

Often, it so happens that when we see a enterprise publishing an commercial enterprise in the newspaper, we anticipate that it's a huge deal to apply and efficiently get into the said agency.

However, you want to preserve in mind the fact that it changed into the enterprise business enterprise that published the want for an worker and now not the alternative way spherical. If they have been no longer in decided want of someone professional, they won't have hit the papers.

The first hurdle has as a cease result been taken care of. You want to keep in thoughts that they want you and no longer the opposite way round. Yes, you too have the want for a interest which will pay, however it's miles their want that overshadows yours. As speedy as you examine the posted name for an interview, you have to mentally put together yourself to capture the opportunity with every your arms.

As toward certainly that specialize in how you'll profits via way of having the employment, you want to understand that occupations are absolutely about imparting some incentive to an affiliation and their customers.

Going into an interview with the outlook of tactics you could offer some incentive to the association permits you to technique the assignment from a totally exclusive attitude altogether.

Many humans, with incessant health situations, typically be stricken with the aid of a lack of self-self notion because of their bodily confinements. And while cash related strain and unpaid payments are introduced to the mixture, the quit end result is an progressed mental pressure. The greater determined you're for artwork, the more scared you could look and become during the interview. You may moreover enjoy inclusive of you need to request or maybe beg for a few component that you need, in preference to offering the use of your talents.

Take a gander at paintings as a honest deal. In this deal, you convert your skills and ability for wages, in return for honest wages and an opportunity to take a look at a few difficulty new. That sounds extra reasonably-priced than absolutely looking on the scenario as being you looking for a method and desperately seeking to go through the interview to get it. You can be amazed that this newly located truth that you have received, honestly with the resource of way of attaining this mere cease, will propel your self-self guarantee.

Organizations are populated thru way of individuals. These people have characters which are regularly related to their company way of life. By doing a touch of studies in advance, you can deal with the important additives in their organisation man or woman. This rapid places you in advance of numerous individuals who are simply searching for a job.

Noteworthy Answers

The maximum common query that is asked at any hobby interview is "Why do you want this method?" Now, you could flow into every way in answering this question; sincere or otherwise. Numerous people will flow on approximately how they want the coins to pay overdue payments, want better fitness advantages or maybe speak how close to the place of work is to their domestic.

If you need to release proper proper into a speech of approaches unpaid payments were surmounting for months and what shape of of a monetary crunch you're in, you will be gambling the sport the sincere way, the without delay way. Despite there being truth observed on this solution, it gained't genuinely cut it. The employer is not inquisitive about the sob tale concerning why you're looking for a challenge. They are extra involved about how you could advantage the capacity business corporation, or what's in it for them.

Another stressful yet critical question usually requested thru employers is, "What are your strengths?" Now, the obvious manner to reply this can be to list all of the strong elements of not genuinely your teachers, however also of your person. However, without a doubt all people else can be doing the identical element. Instead, popularity more on your private developments than the ones already referred to for your resume. By choosing to accomplish that, you are displaying the agency the side of you that has now not been displayed elsewhere. When you show to your employer which you are more than honestly your grades and factors, it instills a religion inside the route of you in them.

Similarly, a whole lot of interviewers ask you approximately your weaknesses. They aren't truely worried to recognise wherein you lack. The primary goal at the back of asking this question is to recognize whether or not or no longer you're self-aware of your weaknesses or not. After being asked about your weaknesses, in case you turn out to be answering with "none," there's a extraordinary danger of you being disqualified then and there. Always be honest even as dealing with this question because, while you're employed, your employers are going to come across your inclined elements except. So, it's miles higher if they're organized to address them, as opposed to unexpected them and dealing with the backlash. Hence, it's far constantly better to be sincere than sorry. It furthermore shows them which you are aware of your weaknesses similarly on your strengths and that's crucial in the workplace.

A genuine CV

A CV is what represents you at the equal time as you are looking for a assignment. It talks approximately you in a manner you wouldn't be able to provide an reason behind in a non-public interview. It is the prima facie proof of your credentials and indicates your functionality to people who are in a characteristic to award you a way. It is of paramount significance which you start strolling inside the direction of building an high-quality CV right out of your pupil days. Interning at correct places, presenting papers to your subjects and working below expert and famend human beings from your challenge, are some of the very giant topics that a competitive CV ought to comprise.

A CV is an legitimate evidence which you personal the considered necessary capabilities to carry out the stated method. There are a few number one matters that have to be sorted within the course of the education of a CV.

The direction that you are pursuing need to be everyday with the pastime which you are trying to find. Choose a course this is collectively with as many tiers as feasible. At instances, the presence of an included diploma rankings you brownie elements, however the fact that the covered person levels may not provide you with a hazard of having you a process, while looked at in isolation.

A top CV additionally has suggestions from all the right places. It is relevant which you intern and advantage experience from human beings and locations that rely and that rise up to the scrutiny of folks that may be interviewing you. If the ones set up within the location declare you're remarkable at your artwork, it counts a top notch deal while you go out on the hunt for jobs. With their backing, you stand extra threat of having the undertaking you need.

It is likewise crucial to apply a clean and legible format. Whoever said seems don't depend in no way found a badly formatted resume. A resume is meant to create a primary effect and a awful layout and incorrect fonts can truely mar your probabilities to even sit down for an interview, not to say land the pastime. Make your resume stand out.

Be honest

A very crucial component that needs to be saved in thoughts even as updating your resume is that lying will subsequently come again to chew your treasured posterior in the long run. Companies regularly have a insurance of taking walks statistics assessments on candidates making use of for a assignment with them. If they locate some thing that's deceptive or even barely unreliable, they may do extra than truly reject your software. Most organizations have a database of lying applicants, which receives shared via the complete regime of groups. The habitual offenders are blacklisted there and then and any employer will will be inclined to go into your name in the database to recognise whether or not or now not you have a statistics of lying in your resumes. Once your name enters the cited database, it's in there all the time. So, being dishonest in your resume will not only quash your present day assignment, but additionally hose down any destiny possibilities you will possibly have.

Proofreading is a have to

Before you put up your resume for a future organization to look at, ensure at least humans go through it for the motive of finding any real or grammatical errors. A smooth typo may also destroy your possibilities to land an interview - for it shows informal approach for your factor.

Do your homework

It is not sufficient that a wonderful CV is produced. It desires to be followed up with the aid of a extremely good amount of research and records exams on the location you're utilising for a undertaking. Getting to realise approximately their records, reputation quo of records, merger policies and wonderful relevant facts about them can are to be had in to be had whilst you're called in for an interview. Being nicely versed with the commercial enterprise enterprise and their nature of labor makes you stand in a fantastic moderate and sends a message to the interviewer that announces you are virtually inquisitive about going for walks with them. It elevates your probabilities of getting decided on whilst you display them how plenty you understand approximately them and their artwork.

The D-Day

An interview is meant to check you on the realistic grounds of the game and recheck the claims you made in the submitted resume. It is of primary importance that your interview goes nicely.

First off, get dressed up properly for the interview. Formals paintings maximum of the time. If any particular coloration or dress code has been requested for, have a look at it to the letter. Do not mismatch your ties and socks and truly do no longer select super and garish colorations that could blind the butterflies. It is favored that you pick somber colored suits to deliver out a glance of professionalism. Also, address your non-public hygiene in advance than taking walks into the interview room. Overgrown beard, dirty nails and filthily on foot noses are organisation turn-offs. They not only score in competition to you, however moreover reflect your personality in society. Someone who's arrived groomed and relevant up like a gentleman is most probable to be preferred over a person who couldn't discover time for some self-improvisation.

Make terrific your posture at the equal time as strolling in, sitting and getting up is, if now not militarily ideal, at the least not in reality well worth of receiving a recoil from the judges. Postures illustrate your technique toward things in stylish. A laid again sitting posture offers off an air of mystery of disrespect, at the same time as one in every of rapt attention offers off effective vibes.

Another very important part of interviews is the manner you speak. The manner you pick out out to talk speaks plenty about you. Use lively and formal language like – "I'd want to discover this possibility" and no longer "Yeah, it'd be proper if I labored with you." While speaking to those undertaking your interview, appearance them in the eye and speak hopefully. Your tone have to signify which you are privy to your abilities and assured approximately them. Guard closer to too much gaudiness and exaggeration at the same time as you're asked to give an reason for your self. Interviews typically begin with a warming up question like "tell us about yourself."

Ensure briefness and quickness in answering this sort of question. They are alleged to make you feel snug earlier than the interview keeps immediately to greater technical questions and discussions. Limit the timing of the answer to such questions to 30 seconds. A quick however inclusive description of your pastimes and qualifications wants to be presented. No one's going to invite further questions on this solution as it's handiest a warming up technique.

Admit your faults

If, in some unspecified time in the future of the interview, you're caught off protect by means of manner of a question which you have not any clue approximately, it's miles negative for your possibilities to head on and on beating throughout the bush than admitting that you don't comprehend the solution. Bluffing attempts by no means initiate the interview conductors. However, an honest "I'm sorry sir, I absolutely have virtually no concept in any way." may also moreover honestly art work on your need. And it moreover offers a bonus in your rating in case you politely ask the conductor the right solution while you've admitted your incompetency.

Companies praise folks that like to analyze and dissent individuals who simply try and faff their way out of a difficult scenario or truely blabber approximately a few detail they don't comprehend the solution to. Your inquisitiveness gets you an thing over individuals who didn't trouble to reply and sulked due to the truth they weren't right at it.

Skill-sets

An corporation generally appears in advance to hiring those who've a essential set of competencies. Some of them are – logical wondering, communique abilties, technical accuracy and interpersonal abilties.

Logical thinking consists of the capability of the human thoughts to arrive at conclusions and take selections based mostly on the power of motive. Inductive, deductive and adductive reasoning capabilities constitute a number one commonplace feel set. Not everyone is capable of wondering logically in terrible situations and sudden times. The better the diploma of common sense decided in a capability worker, the greater his opportunities of having hired.

Communication capabilities are needful to stay on a interest interview. If you aren't capable of deliver your troubles in your business employer and fellow employees in a handy way, then you definately are maximum probably no longer the right man or woman for the mission. An employer-worker courting involves the reporting of sports activities to the agency. Going inside the lower back of the organisation's again or no longer telling him approximately an vital truth that could have an impact on the employer is taken into consideration to illustrate a loss of verbal exchange capabilities.

Technical accuracy is a totally simple requirement. You may be a outstanding human beings person and you can have an

I.Q. Of over one hundred thirty, however in case you fail at getting the technical bolts and nuts right, you're pruned from the start. Being technically well implies getting your fundamentals are sturdy.

A interest at a economic organization may additionally additionally moreover contain being a wizard at accounting and mathematical mumbo jumbo. Or a law company can also need you to be well versed with the usa laws or the charter.

A job is extra than about simply doing art work and getting paid. It has an administrative center and severa distinctive personnel going for walks alongside you. It turns into an unspoken rule to paintings not most effective for the organization, but moreover along side your fellow comrades. An interviewer might be curious to test your social talents with the aid of manner of asking approximately your buddy circle or the manner you spend your leisure hours. Hypothetical questions based on imagined scenarios ought to furthermore be anticipated.

Internships

Internships are a superb manner to get in contact with a enterprise organization even earlier than you begin considering operating for them. An internship now not first-rate gets you referrals, but moreover adjusts you to the artwork surroundings and the manner of life of it. You get to understand fellow personnel and the character in their paintings.

This helps you in identifying in case you want to paintings there or not. Interning at an area may be done at some stage in college holidays or factor time in case your college and place of business allow it. Start off thru volunteering for the art work and ultimately, once they begin noticing your artwork, they may simply pay you for it. Volunteering presentations your determination to the art work. Companies check out their internship field for destiny recruitments. It is a fee-effective technique of making sure the continuance of supplying employment. Interns are preferred over random applicants any day.

Personal contact

If possible, get in touch with the HR of the business enterprise you are inquisitive about walking for. Although it sounds horrible, you can strive the usage of your non-public relationship with them to land a activity in the employer. One shouldn't be embarrassed about accepting a project obtained thru private contacts. After all, that is Darwinism at its fine. The fact which you are known to the human beings hiring you furthermore can also offers you an part inside the interview device, but don't take it as a proper.

Right Approach

Impress the interviewer together with your commonplace sense and cool method. Many interviewers try to trap the candidate off shield with unconventional questions and situations. A hypothetical situation is given and the candidate is asked to reply what he'd do if located in this situation. A cool and humorous method to answering such questions allows your probabilities. Do now not panic and permit the suddenness of the query boggle you. Apply a pinch of not unusual revel in and you will bounce via them.

Take the first step

If you're employed on a trial basis or in case you are an intern - ask for work. It goes within the course of your pastimes which you take a seat at a table all day surfing the Internet due to the fact no art work has been assigned to you. Speak up and ask for paintings. If essential, nag your boss into giving you a few paintings and allow him apprehend you don't want to sit down down idle and vain. Always appear to be you are busy with some element.

Find a assignment that pursuits you

Do now not pass searching out fat paychecks jobs in case you aren't advantageous you'd need to commit some time to the technique in hand. Having skills for a hobby isn't always the same as having the thoughts for it. If you aren't a person who loves to do a secular desk technique, then don't exercise for one. Instead, search for jobs that encourage you to assume outside the cubicle.

Negotiations

The actual talk of your interview takes region typically at the stop of it. This is at the same time as you are requested approximately the remuneration part of the method. The interviewer can also simply offer you with ball park figures. If the interviewer is definitely conveying to you the amount which you need to anticipate, you have not any desire but to just accept it or go away it. This takes place with jobs whose commercials have explicitly mentioned the right reimbursement you may be getting. There is a touch of "no negotiation" on this ad and you should have determined it. It consequently will become unprofessional to even attempt a negotiation in this kind of scenario.

However, if the challenge's commercial or notice had no such factor out of remuneration, it's far implied that they may be inclined to interact you in a negotiation over it. Here are some of the recommendations you want to hold in mind whilst negotiating:

1.   Keep in thoughts your abilities, achievements and enjoy earlier than blurting out an quantity. Your resume need to justify the amount you're quoting. If you quote a few aspect obscenely higher than you glaringly appear to deserve, it is able to put off the interviewer. Likewise, if you quote too low a remuneration, it'll now not handiest be disadvantageous for you, but you will moreover stumble upon as stupid to the ones sitting throughout the desk.

2.   Never quote your compensation amount occupied with your very personal. Always be polite and ask the interviewer about the

charge they count on you deserve based totally mostly on your resume and normal performance in the interview.

3.   If you have were given been knowledgeable a discern which you aren't glad with, particular it in a manner that does not show unhappiness or dissent.

four.   Tell the interviewers approximately your past jobs and what type of you were paid. You can every now and then pick out out to be a piece liberal concerning this parent for the reason that crosschecking sales figures of candidates in their preceding jobs isn't always a ordinary workout. However, play this endeavor with caution as, if determined, it may lead you to get blacklisted.

5.   Always ask if the earnings that is being provided comes with tax-cuts or with out them. Usually, the income that's written into your employment agreement is extra than you absolutely get. This is because of severa taxes, 401(adequate), and distinctive

comparable cuts. Make positive exactly what you've got were given emerge as earlier than you commit.

Chapter 10: Using Body Language

Welcome to the very last bankruptcy of this e-book. In this bankruptcy, we will communicate how you can effectively use your body language and its relevance in interest interviews. You speak with greater than simply words. Your frame speaks even as you aren't paying masses interest and also you with the aid of way of chance become saying plenty about your internal emotions through your body. Though it is in primary terms unintended in nature, you could discover ways to draw close it, so as to use it in your personal advantage in assignment interviews.

Facial Expressions

Your face says lots approximately you. Without treading into the damaging area of first impressions, your face is your whole profile in an interview. It is the primary factor human beings word on the equal time as you stroll into the room. Your mind, your thoughts, your wit, your sense of humor; all come secondary to the onlookers' minds. It is your face that leads everything else.

Droopy eyes surely imply that the man or woman is not interested by what's within the the front of him. It may additionally, at times, additionally be offensive to three human beings. On the opportunity hand, attentive and alert eyes represent which you are without a doubt taking interest what the alternative person has to mention. However, coming out eyes is a sign closer to overacting. If a person's eyes follows the speaker's hand movement, blink at the right time durations and do no longer have eye-sand in them, it leaves inside the again of an first-rate impact on the speaker.

Watch your mouth. Literally! The manner you function your lips in an interview is critical within the course of indicating what temper you are in! If you've got an open mouth, it suggests that each you are dumbfounded through the conversation's contents or you're certainly sitting there not taking note of some thing's being stated. On the opposite hand, in case you use your lips to on occasion smile a touch, it can inspire the interviewer to do greater of what they are doing.

If you are twitching your lips, it shows that you are below a piece of strain. Lip twitching has commonly been associated with tension. If you twitch your lips in a task interview, your opportunities of having determined on drop appreciably, because it indicates a loss of self warranty.

Your eyebrows serve greater purpose than actually completing your face. Use them to finish benefit to show inquisitiveness. You can recognition your eyebrows collectively to signify that you have not understood what has surely been stated. However, an excessive amount of of squinting may additionally backfire, due to the fact it can be overdoing it. You can display 'wonder' via manner of raising your eyebrows, regardless of a great English idiom appointing a wholly particular interpretation to 'elevating eyebrows.'

Express surprise or slight wonder through exploiting your eyebrows nicely.

Your facial expressions cowl extra than absolutely your eyes, lips and eyebrows. It is how your face as an entire is obtainable that topics and no longer just its character elements. When you have a smiling face, it's miles herbal that those sitting right in some unspecified time in the future of the interview desk experience proper vibes coming from you. On the opportunity hand, a face with a grimace on it is taken into consideration bloodless and unfriendly.

Body Postures

Body postures are all approximately the way you carry yourself. It is the very last platform on your body language to be displayed in complete vigour.

Sitting is as important as taking walks. Do not pull the chair out and surely count on that you are to sit down down until someone asks you to. It isn't always first-rate towards your opportunities of landing a assignment, however moreover rude to take a seat down in your non-public as it offers off an air of mystery of superiority. Wait for one of the interviewers to invite you to take a seat down. Assume a immediately posture, along side your backbone touching the again of the chair the least bit elements. Do now not take a seat down too stiff, as that might cause cramps and make you demanding in the end.

Do no longer sit slouching. Straighten up your shoulders a chunk and seem clever at the same time as doing so. Do not pass your legs below the table. Though maximum interviewers cannot see what goes on under the desk, that feature does have an effect on your top frame. One can effects tell how casually your legs are positioned under the table through taking a single study your pinnacle body.

Do now not area one leg above the opportunity at the same time as sitting. It shows which you aren't certainly assured approximately your self, however moreover show a standard mindset of carelessness toward the interviewers. Behave in a way that sends the message that you respect them.

Sitting upright in an interview might possibly flow into in pick out of you as it suggests an attentive mentality. On the opportunity hand, adopting a slouching characteristic suggests that you are inside the temper to pay attention them out and are simplest there best to doodle and pass time.

Gestures

In an interview, in case you are sitting in a flow into-armed characteristic, it implies that you are not welcome to others' point of views and mind. It shows a chilly mind-set and frequently does no longer come off as right. On the possibility hand, in preference to crossing palms, if you sit down together collectively with your arms for your lap or on the desk, you supply off a pleasing and hotter air of thriller and it'll simply fetch you brownie elements.

It is a sign of careless self perception to casually fling your palms round at the same time as strolling. On the alternative hand, if you clench your fists and stroll, it is able to recommend that you are calculated and reserved about your self.

In fine international places, finger gestures may be interpreted in numerous methods. The majority of our planet follows the rule of thumb of thumb of displaying the middle finger to be offensive. On the opportunity hand, in some elements of the arena, it's the show of index finger that's considered aggressive and offensive.

Hands can be used to supply emotions too. Joining your hands in a Namaste signal shows that you advise admire toward the man or woman. Bowing down is some other shape of recognize accompanied via the Japanese. If you display someone the 'thumbs up' sign, it manner which you are each wishing them excellent accurate fortune or are conveying 'ok' or one of its variants. However, in case you do the same in special international locations like Iran or Thailand; it can be taken as an equal of showing the center finger in the West.

So, make sure you do no longer consciously or subconsciously offend your interviewers collectively together with your frame language or gestures.

Handshakes

A very common way to greet each one of a kind is with the aid of shaking each one-of-a-kind's hand. This has been a way of life for the cause that medieval length. A handshake is supposed to suggest greeting, finishing touch, agreement or friendship and calling off of warfare.

In an interview, the number one and handiest physical interaction you will have together along side your potential enterprise is thru the handshake that you carry out while you first stroll in. The way a person shakes his hand with others says lots about him. If the handshake is organization, it way the individual appearing it's miles confident and is apparent about his intentions.

On the other hand, if it's a unfastened handshake, it shows a lack of self-self perception and casualness. A inclined handshake is often taken to be a sign in the course of 1/2 of of-settlement and no longer a whole nod. Studies over time have categorized handshakes into severa instructions just like the Bone Crusher – squeezing palms too hard, and the Limp Fish-weakly completed handshake.

Miscellaneous

Biting your nails is a easy sign of hysteria. Though it's far perfectly human to be concerned, bear in mind it is a rat race competition to be had. Interviewers may be searching out humans that are not going through their private non-public issues already. Hence, it's far truely beneficial now not to chunk your nails and provide them a threat to strike your name off the listing.

Do no longer nod or shake your head at the incorrect instances. In a wholesome of frenzy and a hurry to have an effect on, many candidates fail to even draw near the question and simply nod or shake their head. A nod shows sure and an insignificant shaking of head denotes no. If you have virtually understood the query and are clean and prepared to clarify, only then need to you nod or shake your head. Nodding and shaking of the top furthermore comes under frame language and need to be sparingly used.

Do no longer cringe at a query that has stuck you unaware. It is flawlessly high-quality for a candidate to come upon questions that would baffle them from the very starting. However, do now not make any gesture that announces, 'I am no longer liking this question and I hate you for asking it.'' Instead of flinching or growing a face, act curious and tell them that you haven't any idea regarding the query's answer and would like to recognize the equal.

Tell them that you surrender in spite of trying difficult, and ask if they might offer you with the right answer. Such a gesture places you in an outstanding moderate. It suggests which you have the thirst for understanding.

Make tremendous your toes are located nicely. Feet which can be placed within the course of the door paint a completely sorry photo of a candidate. It suggests that the candidate isn't very keen on bagging the pastime and is sitting there most effective for the sake of acting at the gadget interview. It additionally suggests which you are prepared to walk out any second the interview is over this is obviously not a wholesome sign.

Overview

When referred to as for an interview, make yourself presentable. A fats belly will become presentable whilst followed thru a well-becoming and ironed somber professionalism-oriented blouse and the proper set of pants. Trim, shave and wash earlier than walking in for the interview.

Maintain a top notch posture and talk in a polite way.

Confidence may be advanced with the useful resource of the manner you appearance however don't overdo it. Show them which you are a group character and are willing to take in leadership positions whilst asked to. If requested a few component that flips you out, in desire to freaking out, stay calm and certainly tell them you haven't any idea. Do now not overdo the manner you speak and simply communicate how you may normally communicate together together with your friends. Impress them with your logical clarity, conversation abilties and technical records which might be pre-requirements for the pastime.

Chapter 11: Common Interview Questions

- How did you take a look at this assignment?

- Why do you need this hobby?

- What are your biggest strengths?

- What are your biggest weaknesses

- Tell me more approximately your self?

- What are you the exceptional in shape for this role?

- What are your income expectations?

- Why did you depart your very last activity?

- What are you destiny dreams?

- Tell me about an enjoy wherein you needed to cope with a tough scenario.

- How do you deal with failure?

- How do you address success?

• What makes you stand pleased with the relaxation of the applicants?

• Where do you see your self in five years? 10 years?

• What do you appearance to accomplish in the first 30 days? Ninety days?

• Why are you interested by this enterprise especially?

• What is your best motivation in existence?

• How do you cope with disturbing conditions?

• Tell me approximately a time whilst you disagreed together with your boss or supervisor.

• What do you like the least and the most about this enterprise?

• What are your preferred hobbies and pastimes?

• Are you greater of a frontrunner or a follower? Why?

• Why turned into there a gap in your employment amongst [date] and [date]?

• What are you able to uniquely carry to this agency that others can't?

• If cash wasn't an possibility, what would possibly you do on the aspect of your lifestyles?

• How do you deal with mistakes? Tell me about a time while you probably did.

• What is your unmarried-maximum great accomplishment?

• How would possibly pass about firing someone?

• What is your first-rate art work environment?

• What is your control fashion?

• What is the toughest selection you've had to make inside the beyond 9 months?

- What have become your profits to your previous undertaking?

- What are your top three traits?

- What dispositions would you search for when hiring someone?

- What are our agency values?

- What is our business enterprise's maximum priority?

- What distinctive companies are you considering?

- Have you been fired earlier than? If so, why?

- How might your previous boss and coworkers describe you?

- If you'll be any animal, what could no longer or not it's?

- What is your desired internet site?

- What is your favored ebook?

- What is your preferred mag/magazine?

- What makes you the maximum uncomfortable?

- Are you inclined to journey/relocate?

- Would you be inclined to work forty+ hours each week?

- Would you be willing to paintings on holidays?

- What makes you wake up every morning?

- Do you recognize the call of our CEO?

- If you started out your very own agency, what might probable your top 5 values be?

- Are you right or bad at inquiring for assist?

- What became your college revel in like?

- What had been your responsibilities on your ultimate technique?

- How do you address unresponsive coworkers or clients?

• Tell me about a scenario on the identical time as you have been unsure of the manner to transport beforehand. How did you respond?

• You find out your self strolling on a mission which you cannot complete because of the reality your colleague has now not submitted their paintings. How do you respond?

• Do you make a decision on written or verbal communique?

• What do you do if there is a breakdown of conversation on your group?

• What need to you do if you noticed an worker stealing elements?

• What should you do if any individual took credit in your thoughts?

• How properly do you discovered this interview goes to date?

• Are there any questions that I haven't asked you however?

- Do you've got any questions for me?

Chapter 12: Worst First — Responding to Tough Interview Questions

Let's have a second of honesty right here.

Job interviews may be intimidating and sometimes downright daunting. But right right here's the component: If you have the right technique, mission interviews can be a high-quality learning enjoy and you can clearly have a few fun with them! For now, permit's start with the hardest questions that may be asked of you at a few stage within the interview.

We are addressing those questions first because they may be inclined to make people the most nervous. But if you can paintings via all of the eventualities and plan thoughtful responses, you have to enjoy masses greater possessed in man or woman.

So allow's get it out of the manner by using the usage of reviewing response techniques so you can quell the jitters and bypass on to exclusive assets you need to apprehend so that you can ace that interview.

"What is your excellent weak point?" or "What are your weaknesses?"

Perhaps this is the maximum dreaded interview query ever. It looks like no matter how a high-quality deal you've anticipated it, organized for it, rehearsed your answer countless times, went over the situation for your head (and probable had a dress practice session with a friend further), listening to that query from someone who likely is a stranger can however seize you off-shield.

Why do employers ask those sorts of questions, anyway? The answer is simple: They need to look the manner you'll hold up beneath strain, no longer splendid from the query, however to evaluate the way you've reacted in stressful conditions from the past as nicely.

Here are some hints for addressing this precise query:

1.Discuss a bad trait that can also be considered in a incredible slight. Here are 3 examples to undergo in thoughts:

One inclined factor may be no longer being so suitable at drawing the road among work and the rest of your life. You can add a superb spin to this with the resource of saying which you need to art work extended hours although it's no longer required of you, and though it can have an impact in your art work-existence balance, your ardour and power ensures that you're a diligent worker who is willing to install greater hours need to the need upward thrust up — most employers might be glad to concentrate that. You may additionally even bypass one extra proactive step and say which you are willing to discuss ordinary ordinary performance at your opinions to make sure a sincere and equitable workload for yourself.

Another ability and not unusual prone component is which you're approval-oriented. You can say that you are strongly oriented towards getting into conjunction with all and sundry, however that's simplest because you place a lot rate on camaraderie and teamwork inside the place of job. Stephanie, who fits this description to a "T," says, "It's my personal notion that when colleagues get alongside without a doubt properly with every different, the institution is extra effective and we will be predisposed to generate superior outcomes."

And finally, if you generally generally tend to have a microscopic view of factors at art work, you could tweak your answer to say that you're a perfectionist who loves to double-take a look at his or her paintings. Yes, you may be meticulous, and it is able to appear like you interest at the information too much, however your so-known as fussiness will pay off if your paintings includes paying attention to the brilliant print — fields which includes technological information, remedy, technology, accounting, and so on.

2.Avoid cliché answers.

Your interviewer might want to roll his or her eyes if you use the identical vintage "I'm a workaholic" answer, so do try to remember distinct "weaknesses" you can talk about or as a minimum phrase it more thoughtfully. These can be approximately your preference to be friends with each person, being a perfectionist, or having a aggressive streak.

3.Use common sense on your honesty.

Be practical to your solution. Maybe you're now not a morning man or woman and also you will be predisposed to be grumpy whilst you clock in at art work — in any other case you will be predisposed to be late. It received't do you any suitable to confess this to the interviewer, so avoid citing it. In reality, take an honest observe a number of the ones troubles and ask your self if you are prepared to address and remedy them. Then do it! For the interview, live with the types of developments which can be considered from each elements and you need to be in accurate form.

four.Talk about the way you've managed to address and conquer a weak point.

A right approach, which additionally suggests initiative, is to talk about the manner you've superior for your profession over the years — inclusive of approaches your organizational abilties have been missing, but you've got been capable of improve them by manner of the usage of implementing a device that worked for you, likely coursework or mentorship. Be specific in explaining the manner you've got got been able to deal with such weaknesses. Interviewers will possibly experience if you're now not virtually proper.

Another scenario might be a "weak component" of being so detail-orientated which you commonly have a tendency to spend an excessive amount of time obsessing over trivia and now not concentrating on the massive photo. You can admit this prone factor and proportion the way you have been capable to expose it round with unique steps.

In truth, speakme about the manner you have got been capable to overcome a weak spot want to provoke most interviewers. And it's definitely a extra thrilling respond than the standard, "I like to put in long hours at paintings" or "I'm a workaholic" or "I'm a perfectionist." Just replicate on your past critiques and pick situations in that you probable did the entirety you could to improve yourself.

"What turned into the largest task which you confronted and the way did you deal with it?"

This query is designed to evaluate the manner you've handled demanding situations and problems within the past. It's furthermore a manner for the interviewer to appearance if you have strong trouble-solving competencies, which include initiative, progressive questioning, and resourcefulness.

That said, your answer shouldn't be indistinct. Provide a clean, precise state of affairs and offer an cause behind in detail the manner you dealt with the problem. Let's be smooth:

this isn't an invitation to rant approximately your co-people or your boss. Instead, attention on discussing a in particular hard scenario at art work, and the manner you handled it diplomatically and tactfully.

Some desired instructions to get you wondering encompass:

•A co-worker war you resolved

•How you met goals however restrained time-frame, rate variety, or manpower

•How you addressed market or aggressive threats

•Motivating a flagging crew or unifying a fragmented group

The secret is to emphasise the manner you confronted the challenge, the lessons and realizations you had, and the way you moved in advance to become higher on your artwork. Remember to be concise and now not spend extra than 5 minutes in your reaction.

"What changed into your biggest failure?"

Although it is able to appear to be there's no first rate manner to answer this query, take coronary heart.

People make mistakes all the time at paintings. After all, no man or woman is perfect. In a task interview, this question will assist the interviewer apprehend the manner you view failure, and they may via twist of destiny gauge whether the query makes you cautious or of you answer with calm and poise.

Should you be confronted with this question, bear in mind again the approach for answering the manner you dealt with stressful conditions within the beyond. Emphasize your learning from that revel in and the manner you tried to enhance afterwards.

You don't ought to move into definitely precise info here; without a doubt paint a desired concept of what came about and the manner you resolved it. You may additionally even aspect out how a "unhappiness" resulted in a notable response from you. Describe sure obstacles you've encountered and the way you surmounted them.

Some fashionable mind to get you questioning:

•Failure to recognize at the same time as to stop or transition a task

•A venture that have become not well-researched or nicely-timed for achievement

•Working with an incompatible or poorly built group

•Taking on artwork that grow to be now not for your area of knowledge or energy for the sake of "assisting out"

•Compromising an account because of loss of assist or steering

And in the long run, consider that with a few component you're taking on, on the way to boom your price of success you need to growth your price of failure. Many agile businesses in recent times are incorporating failure into their achievement approach — "the fastest manner to fulfillment is to fail faster." So don't forget this as context for your reply. Mentioning capabilities which embody diligence, willingness to strive some difficulty new, endurance, and perseverance will all artwork on your pick out out.

CHAPTER ASSIGNMENTS:

•Give a few notion to the mission questions on weaknesses, struggle and boundaries. Then consider how every provided you some power, opportunity, or new enjoy that you benefitted from.

•Pick a chum to perform a touch feature-gambling with you so you can experience cushty and snug answering those forms of questions.

Chapter 13: Top 10 Most Common Questions (with Answers)

You've already blanketed the stressful, anxiety-inducing questions, so from here on out you could breathe smooth. You're inside the stretch. The relaxation of the interview questions are going to be masses easier, normally protecting your career evaluations and your personality tendencies.

So now you're equipped to deal with the top 10 maximum not unusual questions and strategize your responses to each. Read them below and make sure to take notes so you can plan and prep your very personal answers, your manner.

1. Tell me about your self.

This question is arguably the most usually posed at the begin of each task interview, and we're able to't pressure this sufficient: stay career-oriented on your answer. The interviewer is not clearly inquisitive about your non-public existence — in that you went on excursion ultimate, what your favored meals is, which musician you want, and so forth. Your solution want to fall within the professional area: which university you name your alma mater and what state of affairs you majored in, your preceding art work tales, and something else that is associated with your line of exertions or profession.

But be careful to maintain your solution concise — don't spend ten minutes occurring and on with none real attention...you don't need to set the verbal exchange adrift even if you are enthusiastic about your severa achievements. Choose your phrases cautiously: Which achievements and employment-associated talents do you want to attention on?

To assist you narrow down the listing, jot down your satisfactory professional developments and look at which ones are fantastic appropriate to the place you're making use of for. The concept is to suit your solution with the competencies and understanding that the corporation agency is looking for.

In fact, a virtually smart technique right proper here is to craft a shape of "elevator pitch" or summary of your career reason: wherein you started out, the essential factor highlights on your expert course, why you're there for an interview and a smooth intention you've got got to your expert future.

A pattern response might be: "I without a doubt have fifteen years' enjoy in small business employer earnings and nearby company manipulate. I'm happiest as soon as I'm on the flow into seeking out new business enterprise. I'm in search of to expand a set to meet assertive marketplace desires through supporting conventional dating-constructing with the current-day in earnings generation."

See how that paints a truely specific and compelling professional image? They'll see that, too, so take a hint time to get your summary absolutely right.

2.What do you undergo in thoughts to be your most significant accomplishment or greatest success to date?

This question is the interviewer's way of gauging your fulfillment at managing people, obligations, your art work, and your self. When formulating your solution, it's first-rate to speak approximately achievements with a view to reveal your strengths and the way your efforts have made a high terrific effect. And once more, don't be vague. Provide information. For example, if the region you're making use of for calls for particular communication capabilities, you may cite times while you settled disputes among co-employees, or how successfully you have been able to rack up sales on your current organization. Use figures and numbers if you could. Don't actually recite the objects for your résumé — the interviewer has already examine your CV so no want to duplicate that.

Instead, select one or key accomplishments that show a whole lot of your abilties. Think of it like a case look at: you started out with "X", used "X and Y" sources, and carried out "Z" outcomes. Of course, it's up to you to fill within the blanks with compelling statistics, so probably top notch to make be aware about it so you are smooth on your message.

three.What are some of your strengths?

Plan your answer such that the strengths you point out (ideally to three) are aligned with the abilities and tendencies favored inside the function you're utilizing for. Elaborate on one in each of them with greater data, using figures or numbers if applicable.

If, as an example, you're making use of for a control characteristic, you can say, "My strengths lie in negotiating, training/mentoring, and project management. I changed into as soon as tasked to educate a fixed of ten new hires for the help desk, and the results showed that their output modified into 20% quicker than their predecessors."

four.Why want to we lease you?

This query lets in your capability employer take a look at your self guarantee on your capabilities and if the ones are applicable to the system you're utilising for. Among all ten questions about this economic disaster, this one is the most apparent opportunity to market yourself, so your "income pitch" need to be aligned with the features the corporation is searching out in an employee.

In enhance of taking walks within the door to your interview, you really need to check the project description and check which capabilities, trends, trends, and qualifications you've got. Choose three which you think are the maximum vital and relevant, and make bigger on every in brief. Don't take extra than minutes to reply — hold in thoughts, this is the equal of a TV business in which YOU are the product being marketed, so your solution need to be concise and straight away to the issue.

5.Why do you need to paintings for us?

Your answer to this query will display your motivations for in search of to sign up for inside the industrial corporation employer. The exceptional course of movement is to research the agency — its project and imaginative and prescient, desires, market regular performance, ancient beyond/statistics, values, way of life, and so forth. (For reference, we cover this subject matter a wonderful deal more intensity with step-via-step detail in the companion ebook "Job Interview Preparation: An Interview Preparation Guide Covering Essentials from Research to a Winning Mindset.")

As you formulate your response, preserve in mind that your reason is to bring how a good buy of an asset you will be to the organisation and the way they'll benefit with the resource of hiring you. Simply positioned, they need to realize what YOU can do for THEM — now not the other manner spherical.

6.Why are you considering leaving your modern-day interest? OR: Why did you stop your very last project?

Be tactful. Perhaps you're sad together together with your contemporary-day process. Perhaps you've got got an unreasonable manager. Perhaps you enjoy absurd office politics every day.

However, this isn't always the time or vicinity to speak about that — you should take the diplomatic course. You can in reality say that your desires and people of your modern business employer don't align. You might also additionally cite that there isn't an opportunity for the sort of professional increase you are searching out. You can also moreover sincerely be excited about a present day concern or new possibilities.

Often we outgrow our jobs, and there is not anything wrong with that.

7.Where do you take a look at yourself 5 years from now?

Employers ask this query for 2 reasons: 1) to look if you are in for the long haul need to they rent you and multiple) to discover in case you are clear about your goals. Your answer should deliver your strain and ambition for non-public and expert boom.

But don't forget to be sensitive to the interviewer's function. You don't need to say you want his or her role, as that would seem threatening. And consider that you don't should respond with some thing that is pick out-precise. Corporate titles change all the time, and they suggest numerous matters in exceptional agencies.

Think rather approximately what you purchased to your skillset, experience, or maybe expert certifications. You can also factor out the forms of agency conditions you desire on the manner to manipulate or deal with within the future.

8.What would your last boss say approximately you?

Be honest! The interviewer will maximum possibly do a history check, and that includes calling up your modern day supervisor to inquire about you. If you and your modern (or most current) boss don't really see eye-to-eye, be sincere however diplomatic at the same time as sharing that.

The nice solution is probably to pick 3 of your amazing artwork developments, and drill down on one in every of them using examples. A precise response might be: "He/she can also need to likely say that I am revolutionary, hard-running, and reliable. I have become the bypass-to worker in fee in their responsibilities once they went on depart or on organization journeys. They constantly delegated projects to me that concerned [list project characteristics]."

nine.Tell us about your duties and duties in your modern-day way.

Again, your solution ought to be honest and direct. Don't exaggerate but don't certainly restate the terms in your résumé. Your answer want to mirror what's for your résumé but you may upload greater element and personality past what is at the found out net web page.

One approach is to cover 3 to 5 key responsibilities and as you percentage them one-through-one, communicate in short approximately why every responsibility is a tremendous in shape for you and what you enjoy about it.

10. What are your income expectations?

This question can be a touchy difficulty for a number one interview, but is a excellent get right of entry to into reading the manner you view your truly worth, professionally speakme.

There are situations in which this question can rise up, which may moreover affect your reaction to it.

Scenario One: The business enterprise has already made diagnosed both an hourly fee or a income range for the location you're inquisitive about.

Response: You can say that your revenue or profits expectations are in keeping with the range that has been supplied, and which you appearance in advance to discussing specifics ought to you be the selected candidate for the vicinity.

Scenario Two: The earnings rate or income variety for the region has no longer been disclosed.

Response: This within reason common. Many interest postings have the indistinct "profits commensurate with experience" disclaimer. An worker is an fee to the agency commercial enterprise company, so the concept is to strike a stability amongst profitability and equity. Never fear, proper here is how you may respond to this question.

Do a touch homework. You can go to websites which includes profits.Com, payscale.Com, or salaryexpert.Com and conduct comparative research on revenue degrees that appropriate for your intended function and area.

The important component to phrase even as answering this query is being careful now not to shortchange yourself. As long as you could provide an explanation for your motives at the back of the amount (you have tenure, above-common skills, the living prices are extra costly inside the place you're moving to, and so forth.), don't be shy about mentioning a determine that clearly represents what you're properly properly worth.

In each state of affairs, you're without a doubt inside your right to say that you'd be glad to talk approximately repayment specifics as speedy as you are each a finalist or the chosen candidate for the location.

CHAPTER ASSIGNMENTS:

•Go over every of those questions thoroughly. Use a digital record or a notepad to put in writing out your mind on every.

•Get a honestly easy, concise precis of what your largest promoting factors are relative to this function. Make a trouble to consciousness on as a minimum three traits. Here are some examples: top notch assignment manage, progressive wondering, examined salesmanship, and powerful team manage.

•Do your earnings studies. Even in case you are quite fantastic about your profits or income, you have to virtually do some contextual research on your area so that you are in a better position to talk approximately the problem want to it rise up inside the interview, or negotiate it later ought to you be furnished a position.

Chapter 14: Seven Additional Popular Questions (moreover with Answers)

In addition to the 10 maximum usually asked questions in hobby interviews cited in the preceding bankruptcy, there are nevertheless a group of different well-known questions that employers usually pose. Here is a list of greater not unusual questions and some guidance on a manner to answer them.

IMPORTANT NOTE: The questions beneath are regular regardless of place or enterprise. If you in reality want to ace your manner interview, spend a while bobbing up with questions focused to your place of hobby (e.G. Income, public family members, pharmaceuticals, medicine, and so forth.). Get a colleague that will help you brainstorm and expect which specific questions can be raised in the path of the real interview.

Remember: the extra time you may decide to be inside the area of those questions and answers, the extra relaxed you can experience even as you're being interviewed, as a way to allow you to reveal up more authentically and with extra self belief.

1. What do you realize about our enterprise?

Employers ask this question because of the fact they need to recognise in case you are truly interested in working for them — and if you're willing to move the more mile by using using doing all your homework. So examine up on the industrial company employer! Check out the enterprise net site, get comments from your contacts approximately the enterprise, and scour the information pertinent to the employer. The interviewer can be stimulated by using manner of how an lousy lot you recognize, and don't hesitate to sneak in a reward about certainly one among their awards or new purchaser acquisitions.

(While this e-book focuses generally on questions and solutions, we do cowl extra on research inside the accomplice e book "Job Interview Preparation: An Interview Preparation Guide Covering Essentials from Research to a Winning Mindset.")

2. Are you inclined to excursion? Are you inclined to relocate?

These questions are designed to gauge how bendy you are. If you declare to be simply passionate about your career and professional increase, then the idea of traveling and moving shouldn't trouble you.

However, if you discover yourself in occasions at the same time as journeying and relocating aren't an alternative (e.G. You have a circle of relatives that you may't simply up and skip from one place to every other), be honest and give an explanation for why you may't. You can also say that you are open to locating some center floor that meets every your and the employer's desires.

three. Would you maintain in thoughts your self a pacesetter or a follower?

There isn't always any right or incorrect answer right here. The interviewer without a doubt desires to recognize which magnificence you apprehend your self to fall below. Do some soul-looking earlier than the interview and excellent-track your answer. There are also a whole lot of career-oriented character checks which incorporates Myers-Briggs, which will let you get higher in touch along with your personality profile.

Whatever your orientation, it's likely nice to beef up your answer with examples that highlight the exceptional aspects of being a pacesetter or a follower (e.G. Mentoring and motivation for manipulate, and the rate of teamwork with the useful resource of using being a follower). Additionally, there are wonderful situations in which you can play both position, so you can factor out that you are high-quality at being both and it truly is predicated upon at the state of affairs.

four. What are your hobbies?

Often, interviewers ask this out of sheer hobby or as a do not forget of ordinary; however every now and then, this question may be directed to discern out in case you'll combination properly with the group and suit in with the organisation lifestyle. So take that into consideration whilst considering your solution here.

Consider this case. Linda, a women's mag editor, says asking this particular query is a must each time she displays applicants due to the fact "I need to choose whether she will relate to the topics we cover. If the applicant is not into popular subculture, has no concept approximately style traits or ladies's problems, it acquired't be a super in shape. I need someone who is aware of our marketplace and our readers."

Also endure in thoughts bringing up any hobbies that tie into the popular developments for your supposed interest function. For instance, in case your obligations require you to be element-orientated, and also you paint landscapes for your spare time, you can component out that you truly enjoy the method of placing sensible touches on even the smallest issue of your painting. As every different example, in case you are making use of for a position at a begin-up company, and you're an avid skier, you can effortlessly tie on your love of speedy-paced adventure, it's a outstanding in shape for a trendy corporation.

5. When are you able to begin?

Don't jump to conclusions definitely but! Just take this query at face value and answer truly; employers commonly will ask this as a way to take note of your availability, however it doesn't routinely endorse which you're at the shortlist.

And in case you are presently hired, please ensure that you may supply suitable enough be aware – notwithstanding the fact that your new organisation may additionally moreover need you on their institution as fast as possible, they will furthermore appreciate that you don't want to depart your contemporary organisation at a loss with the aid of a unexpected departure. Make remarkable to be perfectly honest...you don't want to be provided a role and then alternate begin dates due to something you hadn't shared so be perfectly clean on this earlier than you're taking a seat down for the interview.

6. Do you have got were given got any questions for me?

Most interviewers will invite you to show the tables because the interview starts offevolved to wrap up. The worst element you could do is to say that no, you don't have any questions — it can deliver the effect that you're either in a rush to complete up the interview or don't have something to make contributions.

Instead, plan in advance and use this possibility to invite clever, nicely-crafted questions in case you want to precise your right hobby within the hobby and the organization. Not to fear – Chapters 4 to 7 will offer you with precise tips on which questions you should and have to now not ask.

7. What do you need high-quality and least about running in this enterprise?

As for what you want notable approximately your company, take a chunk time to summarize proper down to 1 to a few key factors. This is really the time to be sincere about whether or no longer or now not you thrive on a changing surroundings, experience meeting new human beings, or like to live at the main fringe of era. All of the characteristics that you proportion will advocate a few component about your character and what you may be bringing to the commercial enterprise company.

Note that the implication inside the second part of that question may moreover locate any horrible feelings and mind you will probably have approximately your profession. The fantastic response might be to position greater emphasis on what you really like and characteristic a favored answer for what you don't like. For example, "As an marketing and advertising and advertising government, I like assembly new people and honing my creativity, but it does require being alert to dynamic market changes."

CHAPTER ASSIGNMENTS:

•Go over every of those questions very well. Use a virtual record or a notepad to jot down out your thoughts on each.

•Brainstorm five-10 extra questions which may be precise in your scenario or business enterprise. If you get caught in this, ask a depended on colleague that will help you reflect onconsideration on a few alternatives. Chapter four: The Importance of Asking Smart Questions

This might not be proper for you, however it's far proper for lots human beings: manner interviews create anxiety — tension about performing smart, organized, and best.

Unfortunately, feeling this shape of anxiety can make us 100% focused on "prevailing" — ensuring we make a high-quality have an impact on irrespective of what. And while there's nothing incorrect with making an great have an effect on, it can be easy to forget about that YOU are also there to interview THEM.

Let that sink in for a minute...this is YOUR interview, too!

Additionally, asking questions:

•Demonstrates which you are interested in the interest and organization

•Increases your connection to the interviewer

•Gives you a far better concept of the process and duties

•Can assist distinguish you from first rate interest applicants

•Demonstrates that you are assured enough to take fee

•Gives you an same voice in the interview

Your time and your talents are treasured -- undergo in thoughts which you are looking for the awesome in form thinking about an splendid way to be to absolutely everyone's benefit (and make you happier in the long run).

There are an endless huge sort of questions to ask but you most probably have a restrained time with the interviewer — usually approximately an hour. The following couple of chapters will cover key questions inside the maximum applicable classes to assist manual you on which questions are the pleasant to be able to ask. Remember to honor the interviewer's time and prioritize your questions earlier than you arrive.

We advocate which you jot down the questions you need to invite and take them with you into the hobby interview.

Any questions however? No? Good.

Because you're about to get some thoughts...make sure to be aware of your favorites.

Chapter 15: Sample Questions to Ask the Interviewer: The Job and The Team

Think of the hobby interview as a number one date – you are surely studying every different to peer if there can be a opportunity of a continued courting. The interviewer has completed with their questions and now it's your turn. Just if you are wringing your palms about the revenue and remuneration bundle deal, now isn't always the time to ask how huge your workspace or place of business can be or what number of days of vacation you'll be entitled to if you're employed.

Instead, take this opportunity to show off your smarts and ask about the method and the human beings you'll be on foot with. After all, in case you're going to be spending about forty hours every week with a particular group of people, it might be good to understand in case you'll suit in nicely with them, right? As lots due to the fact the interviewer, you moreover mght want to realize in case you're the right fit for the surroundings.

Here are some pattern questions you may ask:

"Perhaps you could describe a median day at art work?" or "What is a median day within the workplace like?"

With this query, you may get a current day idea of the workflow and the tempo of the project. You may also even get a deeper information of the responsibilities and obligations of the area you're utilising for. Don't be afraid to dig deeper with reference to duties and particular responsibilities — you'll be the excellent doing them anyways!

"Who is the perfect candidate for this pastime?"

The strategy to this query serves competencies. First, you'll be capable of test out when you have the abilities and tendencies had to fill the location. This could be very crucial due to the fact the location that you'll be pleasurable can be an critical trouble in your desire-making way. Second, you'll have a sympathetic view for the interviewer's mindset, evaluating your unique strengths and enjoy with what they may be looking for.

"Who will I be on foot with?" or "Can you describe the group or human beings I'll be running with?"

Professional rapport and camaraderie is vital even as it comes work productiveness and satisfactory output. You need to apprehend in case your character will mesh well with the humans you're going to be going for walks with. Most importantly, do ask about your boss or manager, on the grounds that she or he may be the only in rate of your future at artwork!

Don't be afraid to ask approximately specifics, along side drilling down into group dynamics, or maybe asking approximately how regularly the group meets or how the organization's goals are set and how frequently. In some cases, the agency plans on a chain of interviews, and in case you pass "Round

One," you can in truth get a risk to meet your meant colleagues. In truth, you may really ask if the finalist applicants can also have an possibility to meet the team.

Separately, don't forget that the group need to paintings as a unit but additionally understand and play to man or woman strengths...any data you could get from the interviewer will assist you count on what the paintings dynamic is and the manner you wholesome in with it.

CHAPTER ASSIGNMENTS:

•Really bear in mind what's most essential to you regarding the activity role you're utilising for. Give some idea in your employment records and specific annoying situations similarly to possibilities that offer an incredible context in your priorities. Select the maximum essential 1-three questions for this.

•Think about your employment statistics and the evaluations you've had along side your near co-personnel. Prioritize 1-3 questions to help you higher understand the organization you'll be strolling with.

Chapter 16: Sample Questions to Ask the Interviewer: Company and Culture

As with the previous monetary destroy, it's critical to recognize the ins and outs of the company — the working surroundings, the way of life, the folks who lead it. Says Jeanne, who's had a a success career in advertising and marketing and advertising and marketing however needed to pass through numerous organizations in advance than settling together with her cutting-edge employer (which she's been with for the beyond five years), "Sometimes, it's now not pretty plenty you. Sometimes, it may be approximately them. It's critical to find the right in form and find the employer that aligns alongside aspect your desires and vision."

So use your flip as "interviewer" to invite the ones organisation-related questions:

"How might probably you describe the commercial enterprise business enterprise's manipulate fashion?"

Some companies are very strict with sure rules, on the same time as others are pretty casual. Asking this question will will let you recognize about how the organization is run, and you'll have a higher gauge as to whether or not or no longer that style works for you.

You can also drill down into asking similarly approximately the control – does manage meet quarterly and hand down their dreams and vision therefore? Or is the enterprise organisation more organically controlled? Success comes from the top, so it is vital that permits you to understand the control style and practices.

"What do you need approximately working on this corporation?" or "What's it want to paintings in this organisation employer?"

Listen cautiously to what the interviewer has to say. He or she has tenure within the company and may offer treasured insights approximately what it's need to be hired within the employer. If he or she is genuinely obsessed with the operating surroundings and the human beings she works with, you could ask additional questions to delve deeper. Their solutions will provide you with a clearer photo of whether you percent the company's vision, task, and way of life.

However, if the interviewer is suffering to find out some factor powerful to mention approximately walking for stated organisation organisation, it need to clue you in that it could not be the high-quality place of business for you.

What are you capable to tell me approximately the corporation way of life?

What you're searching out proper here is to get a sense of wherein the industrial corporation organization surroundings is like almost approximately polarities like formal vs. Informal, installed vs. Bendy, conventional vs. Revolutionary. The interviewer can also supply examples of enterprise retreats, corporation occasions, or maybe typical overall performance protocols. You can and must ask a approximately any of those orientations which is probably important to you. E.G. Is the company family-great? Does the enterprise organisation spend money on its personnel with expert improvement and schooling applications?

You also can ask about how new merchandise are evolved, how the customer support philosophy is performed, or similar problems that higher display screen how the economic employer commercial enterprise organisation operates.

Chapter 17: Questions to Avoid – Best to Wait

Even although you're given a flip to be the inquisitor, there are high-quality questions that might not be appropriate for the number one interview. Ultimately you should use your very personal judgment, and keep in thoughts that despite the fact that you could not cover those devices first of all, you can clearly deal with them even as a assignment provide has been made.

The following can be sensitive first-interview subjects:

Salary. If possible, wait until after an offer is made. Don't carry up the hassle of cash besides the interviewer does so. There are many elements that pass into negotiating income and income, so it's virtually OK to take care of get in addition alongside inside the interview gadget and you are extra knowledgeable about factors wherein you can negotiate.

Benefits, medical medical health insurance, 401K, and unique perks and privileges. You CAN ask casually about those, but you needn't get into all the facts. Wait till you get the pastime offer earlier than addressing all your blessings questions. It's possible that they may have a Human Resources advantages records packet, or can set up for a conversation amongst you and HR to address all your inquiries. The first interview is ready assessing in form and just consider which you don't want to lessen into any time so that it will assist them gauge your strengths.

Working from home or telecommuting. If the manner records didn't specify some issue in this hassle matter, it's wonderful to wait till you've got got a assignment provide to your arms. There are many, many processes to negotiate working from domestic (we can be addressing that during a separate e-book!) however it's exquisite to comprehend that the agency in truth desires you on board in advance than broaching that difficulty.

Promotions and increases. To keep away from giving the have an impact on which you're perhaps a piece too keen to move on in advance than you've even started out, you want to exercise decorum about this issue rely, and dispose of to a 2d or next interview. One manner you may navigate that is thru asking approximately the procedure of average overall performance opinions -- but keep the thoughts-set of asking to higher understand the protocols. Are reviews performed quarterly? Annually? By buddies? Just do not forget that you don't look like extra inquisitive about the "subsequent pass" than in contributing to the location you are interviewing for.

Time off and holiday leave. Jumping proper into this could make you appear like you're ready to take off from artwork and start planning your vacation the minute you're employed. Again, wait till a proposal has been made earlier than asking. At that element, it's absolutely suitable to inform the company of time without work that you have already dedicated to (a family tour, for example).

Any bad press or rumors approximately the organisation. If you haven't showed some issue and don't have information to decrease back it up, without a doubt don't point out it. In truth, if you have decided some bad press about the employer, it's sincere to assess whether or not or now not it's an top notch suit for you. If it's not, simply exercise somewhere else!

CHAPTER ASSIGNMENTS:

•Make have a look at of some topics you need to cowl for any possible follow-up interviews that you'll be invited decrease lower back for.

•Also make phrase of any deal-breakers or key objects (brought about through manner of using the gadgets above) which you need to cover inside the case that you do get hold of the hobby offer.

Chapter 18: After the Interview...Following Up

How important is a study-up?

Incredibly important.

Don't make the mistake of assuming that when you leave the ball is inside the interviewer's court docket. Or that they'll be too busy to have a look at your questions or thank-you be conscious. Consider that if you pass the more mile, i.E. Writing or sending a thank-you word or e mail for granting you an interview, you can likely differentiate your self from the shortlist in their finalist applicants.

Why is following up so critical? Here are 3 key motives:

1.It reinforces your interest and exuberance within the function.

Take this possibility to emphasize, in writing, why you recollect that you are the proper character for the task. Aside from bringing up how an awful lot you recognize the interviewer's time, your be aware can also carry mind you may have on what else you may deliver to the present day group or undertaking.

2.It shows you're confident.

A thank-you examine emphasizes which you are prepared to begin and are searching forward to the subsequent conversation together along side your capability employer. With a easy be aware, you're already maintaining your self as a strong candidate for the area.

three.You'll get determined.

Consider writing person thank-you notes to each interviewer and use the take a look at as an possibility to similarly spotlight your interest inside the function, and factor out anything important which you failed to mention sooner or later of the interview, which include your mind and hints.

It's moreover in reality appropriate to consider some item that modified into stated at some degree inside the interview and addressing it for your be conscious. Or, doing more industrial agency corporation or commercial enterprise organization studies and sending the interviewer a relevant statistics article – this could in reality make you stand out as having initiative and being proactive.

The Thank-You Note

Make sure that your be aware is properly-written, clean, and concise — the functionality to get right to the component will store the interviewer from having to scroll through rambling pages which might lose their hobby.

Edit and proofread it at least two times earlier than sending it out, and bear in thoughts having a relied on colleague evaluation it for you. Avoid slang and using exclamation elements. You need your letter to be expert and polished. Remember, you're writing to a ability enterprise, not a friend or relative.

It may be a big improve if you could ship the word the day of the interview itself. However, if that's now not possible, deliver one the next day. The rule is: the sooner the better.

Lastly, preserve in thoughts that the have a look at is not a recap of the manner certified you're, however about the interviewer and his or her kindness for offering you with a window of opportunity thru the interview, and any applicable comply with-u.S.A. Of americato the discussion.

Here is a pattern of a extraordinary thank-you notice:

[Subject] Thank you in your time and subsequent steps.

Dear Ms./Mr. [full name of interviewer],

Good afternoon. I truly loved my time with you this morning and I favored to tell you that I am thankful for the opportunity to speak about my skills and provide an motive for my interest within the feature of [insert job title here] in [company name]. After discussing extra information with you, I see myself as a superb healthy for the location and invite you to attain out have to you have were given any greater questions for me.

[Optional] Separately, I were considering our speak about [topic] and decided the subsequent article very applicable to our speak. I want you enjoy it [link to news article].

Thanks once more on your time and attention this morning, I really understand some time and sit up straight for paying attention to from you speedy.